Praise for
MOMENTS IN TIME

"*Moments In Time* is a charming collection of vignettes taken from various points in the author's life, from childhood to maturity. Often touching, sometimes funny, these stories are never dull, invariably entertaining and sure to leave a smile on your face."

~Michael B.

"Amanda Grove Holmén's life has been anything but ordinary. *Moments in Time* is proof – a fun, engaging must-read."

~Annika A.

"Amanda writes with heart-warming honesty, taking the reader on an unforgettable journey with her first book, *Moments in Time*. It will make you laugh, cry, and fall in love with her writing. Always poignant. Often funny. Amanda will capture your heart with her candor and wit in these well-written stories."

~Anneliese O.

"While reading *Moments in Time*, I felt as if I was having a conversation with Amanda - full of laughter, memories, honesty and candid acknowledgement of regrets and mistakes. I could feel how each interaction affected her, as if I were there with her. Amanda's memoirs remind us that you can experience many difficult, even heart-rending, situations with family, friends, and professional colleagues, and still laugh, even at yourself. I highly recommend reading it."

~Janet M.

MOMENTS IN TIME

A Collection of Memoirs

AMANDA GROVE HOLMÉN

Schuler Books
Chapbook Press
2660 28th Street SE
Grand Rapids, MI 49512
(616) 942-7330
www.schulerbooks.com

Moments in Time

ISBN 13: 9781957169835

Library of Congress Control Number: 2024908780

Certain names and identifying details have been changed in this book. Pseudonyms include: Elliott, Laura, Stanley, Jim, Ryan, Hank Shine, Josh, Kelly, and Raj.

Cover Art by Amanda Grove Holmén, 2010

Printed in the United States.

Author's Note

    This collection of memoirs was written from January 2017 through May 2019 for a weekly women's memoir writing class at the Cosmopolitan Club in New York City. The memoirs appear in the order in which they were written and not in chronological order. The collection spans decades of memories from childhood through adulthood. Topics include: family, school days, dating, career, marriage, children, parenting, friendships, passions, adventures, misadventures, lessons learned, life philosophies, love, and loss. Each memoir captures a moment in time. In reading the collection, it is my hope that the reader will come to know me better; just as I have through the process of writing it.

New York City
June 25, 2019

Table of Contents

To Rob, Grey and Ford,

With love and thanks

for keeping me securely rooted in the present

and looking toward the future,

while exploring my past.

Don't You Dare

*D*on't you *dare*," my mother hisses at me.

We are on vacation on the Big Island of Hawaii, staying at the home of a colleague of hers at the law firm. It's the mid-1970s. We are saving money by staying there, instead of at the usual hotel on the other side of the island. We are all uncertain of how to stay in this house, with a very rocky, very crowded, black-sand beach outside the door.

Supermarket food is stacked in the refrigerator, there's no swimming pool, and, worst of all, torrents of rain are falling today as they have for many days now. The house is dark and gloomy. My sister, brother and father are all somewhere else inside the house, likely feeling morose as well. I'm sitting on a high stool at the kitchen island with my mom. I'm twelve years old. My feet swing at least a foot above the brown linoleum floor. A light bulb hangs from a fixture above us, giving the room a sickly, yellow glow. It's late August.

My mom takes a long drag on her cigarette and blows upward. I watch the gray cloud of smoke rise from her parted lips and hover under the light.

"Mom," I say. "Please stop smoking." I'm looking up at her. I love her. I know that smoking isn't healthy. We talked about it in my science class at school. My teacher says it might even cause *cancer*. Even the word scares me. I don't want her to get sick and die.

My mom is tall, thin, blond and, sitting there in that kitchen, dead calm. She's not reacting to my plea. She continues to smoke as though I'm not there. Maybe she's thinking about my request? I can't tell. The plumes of ugly smoke continue to fill the dim room. I feel sick. The stench clings to me – my clothes, my hair. The metal ashtray sits in front of her on the island, full of coils of ash and lipstick-stained butts. More moments pass. Then finally she smiles and looks down at me but there's anger behind her eyes and she speaks in a diabolical sounding whisper.

"Don't you *dare* ask me that again or else there will be no new school clothes for you *this year*."

I feel my heart constrict. Dread. Fear. Panic. My pre-adolescent, grade-school self loves the ritual of shopping for new school clothes. My wardrobe is vital to my self-confidence and my sense of self. I breathe in the stale stink of smoke, defeated. My mom has chosen an ominous punishment intended to hurt. What choice do I have?

"Okay," I say, and slither off the stool.

Petra

*J*osefina Contreras Gomez or "Petra" as everyone called her, was a force in my life. She came to live with us when I was about two years old. Petra hailed from Ayutla, a town in the state of Jalisco in Western Mexico. She was the second eldest in a family of eleven girls: three died young, five were nuns, two weren't, and then there was Petra – the life-long virgin. Devoutly Catholic, she arrived in the San Francisco Bay Area in the 1960s at the age of 50 or so. Through a distant cousin, she landed a job with my family as a nanny, and stayed for twenty years. She spoke only Spanish, pretty much. My mom spoke high-school Spanish and my dad spoke none. The family consisted of my parents, three kids, ages one, two and four, and two Siamese cats.

Onto the scene came Petra, my very own Hispanic Mary Poppins. She had short, straight, jet-black hair, which she cut in a boyish style and dyed herself. She bore pockmarks all over her face from having endured small pocks as a child. She was about 5' 5" tall, and stocky. Her skin was dark and leathery. Her daily uniform never varied: a skirt, a sensible short sleeve blouse and a cardigan. Completing the look were knee-hi stockings and the practical, sturdy, lace-up, black squared-toed shoes that nurses, the elderly, and nuns wear. To fortify the knee-hi, Petra added her own twist: a pair of regular elastic bands just below the top rim. Then she folded the top inch of the stretchy tan fabric over the elastic bands.

Add to that outfit a simple, ever-present crucifix, and you get the picture.

Petra was my favorite person from the get-go. As soon as I could walk, every night at some point I woke up and I made my way through the labyrinth of our Mediterranean home, down the curving stairs and hallways in the semi-dark, stealth as a burglar, to Petra's room off the kitchen. It was an adventure. I believe Petra left a few lights on to guide my passage. It was my very own pilgrimage to Mecca – only my shrine and safe harbor were Petra's warm bed and welcoming embrace. She would wake up and good-naturedly lift up a corner of the covers on her twin bed. I would then crawl in beside her, and inhale the soothing smell of Vick's VapoRub, which she dabbed into her nostrils as part of her nightly ritual. Oh, how I loved the smell! To this day, to open the familiar jar with its turquoise cap and inhale the vapor, conjures her in my mind and heart. At some point, though, my parents didn't approve of my nightly excursions, and decided to take matters into their own hands. Unbeknownst to me, one night they turned off all the lights. On that fateful night, I took a wrong turn and ended up howling and traumatized in a corner somewhere at the other end of the house from Petra's room. I'm not sure how it was resolved among them, but from that night forward the lights remained on and I continued to visit Petra uninterrupted.

The nocturnal rendezvous were only the beginning. As I grew, Petra became "Petrita" to me, and I became "Amandita" to her. Just like Don Quixote and Sancho

Panza, Petrita and Amandita were inseparable. The relationship wasn't complex: I was always getting into trouble, and she was always getting me out of it. When I broke things, she fixed them. When I made a mess, she cleaned it up. Looking back, I see that my antics were akin to those of "Ramona the Pest," a favorite childhood heroine in one of my books. My capers were frequent.

The fate of my sister Allison's brand-new scale with a "Charlie the Tuna" picture on the top was a perfect example. It was one of her birthday presents when she turned nine. She loved weighing herself but wouldn't let me use it. I was almost 7 at the time. I decided to take matters into my own hands. I took it when she wasn't there and started moving the tense, adjustable dial at the top up, up and up, from zero past 50lbs, then 100lbs and higher. Suddenly the spring gave way with startling "PINGGGGGG!" Who did I run to? Petra. How she fixed that thing I will never know. She did though, and Allison was none the wiser.

Petra was part cleaning woman, part nanny, part cook and part disapproving religious presence. By 1975, both my parents were professionals; my father was a doctor, and my mother was a lawyer. Neither was home during the day. From grade school until I left for college, it was Petra who was home. To say there was very little supervision is putting it mildly. That alone made us popular with our peers. Ours was a favorite home to visit. My friends loved the unlimited sugar snacks. We boasted arguably the best snack drawers in the neighborhood. All kinds of sugared cereals, as well as Ho Hos, Pixy Stix, and

Pop-Tarts filled those drawers to the brim. But even those snacks could not compare with the cooking experiments that took place on a regular basis in our kitchen. My personal favorite ingredients were always baking soda, baking powder, and food coloring. My grade-school self, as well as a friend or two usually, concocted gigantic green muffins that stretched the limits of the paper-lined muffin tins that failed to contain them. It was always a thrill to push the oven light on and see how close I could get to blast off! When I wasn't exploding colorful foodstuffs, I was baking homemade chocolate chip cookies or making Oreo-crusted, Baskin-Robbins' Jamoca Almond Fudge ice cream cakes with chocolate sauce topping.

These cooking extravaganzas took place around 3:30pm, right after school. I'd be in the kitchen, and Petra would retire for some well-deserved R and R. By the late afternoon the house was always toasty, basically set to her native temperature, and Mexican music would be playing. Petra would lie down on her back on one of the long, yellow silk living room sofas. I can picture her in repose: her arms cradling the back of her head, which rested on a throw pillow, her legs crossed at the ankles, revealing the inch of skin between her knee-highs and skirt.

Undoubtedly, a good amount of prescription Valium was involved in these siestas. She was a devoted fan. Her two "non-nun" sisters, who lived in Mexico, it seemed to me had almost single-handedly populated the San Francisco Bay area. Petra had loads of nieces living nearby that were wreaking havoc with their lives, and hers. At any given moment, she had to deal with drug arrest, prison stints, car accidents, requests for money, out-of-wedlock babies, as well as a host of other issues -- as the only aunt living in the vicinity of these young women. They drove her crazy. She was a moral pillar who struggled to deal with the disappointment of all these chaotic and constant problems. Her solace: God and Valium. Every day she went to church and prayed and, I would venture to guess looking back, every day she took a bit of Valium religiously. As I got older, it made perfect sense to me. And, really, who could deny her that? Certainly not my parents given that everything looked in order when they returned home. She had the patience of a saint, in large part a product of her living better through pharmacology. Petra took it all in stride, even my crazy kitchen fiascos. And, I'm embarrassed to say now, she cleaned them all up too. If that weren't bad enough, I wasn't the only one making a mess: my brother and sister also found fascination in experimental cooking. So maybe the need for Valium wasn't solely because of *her relatives.*

It was a colorful household to say the least. Visiting flocks of nuns, free-spirited and misguided young nieces, warm temperatures and Mexican music, all combined to form a cultural and linguistic microcosm unlike those of most of my sheltered peers. Even the lowlights are now highlights in retrospect. One of the coolest things was Petra's car: a 1950s style Comet. It had wings, leather seats, and a huge, glossy steering wheel. It was pristine and went through many years of various paint colors. Young men were always approaching her on the street trying to buy it. She loved to say no, shaking her head, but I could see the hint of a smile. She was proud to own such a sought-after pair of wheels. She confided in me one day that she knew the "cholos" wanted to buy the car to race it. But as a young girl, I found it mortifying whenever she picked me up in her car at my elementary school. I much preferred to take the bus. Here's why: it was 1970, in an affluent Northern California suburb and I was a 6-year-old girl. Every day at 3 o'clock, a sea of station wagons (and even some Mercedes and Cadillacs) arrived with (to my mind) uniformly pretty, preppy, normal-looking moms driving them, coming to pick up their kids. Now, imagine Petra in a wide-brim sombrero honking the horn of her shiny tan Comet while cruising up the driveway and roundabout in front of my elementary school. I died a thousand deaths. I never understood why she added insult to injury by honking all the way up the driveway. "*Hola, Amandita*!" she'd shout out the window to me, waving enthusiastically as she came to a halt. I'd sprint to meet her, get in the car as fast as I could, and slouch down in the front seat flushed and embarrassed. "Meet me down the block next time," I begged her more than once. She never did.

A Month of Silence

*S*he got into the yellow cab. "Where are you headed, lady," the driver asked gruffly, looking straight ahead. A few seconds passed and then a few more. In frustration he turned his head to look at her. She shrugged, smiled wanly and pointed to the child's magic eraser board she held in her hand. It read, "80 and Park please," in dark print scrawled on the white plastic background. His brow unfurled as he realized this wasn't an ordinary passenger. "Ok, sure," he said gently, as he drove away from the curb.

I was that silent woman. It was July 2005. A few days earlier, I'd been diagnosed with vocal cord polyps. My kindly, grey-haired, ear, nose and throat doctor told me that my vocal cords were bleeding, and that if I were really good and stopped talking that *instant*, I could have surgery two weeks later. That, he said, would be my reward for shutting up *immediately*. And, if that surgery happened, he continued, I would need to stay quiet for at least two *additional* weeks post op. *Some reward*, I thought to myself.

"You mean starting right now?" I croaked.

"Yes, right now," he said.

Thus began my month of silence.

For a few months prior to that fateful appointment, I'd been experiencing random hoarseness. My throat felt a little sore too. I was a television news anchor in New York City at the time. Several times, while on-air, suddenly it sounded as though a frog was caught in my throat. It was distressing, but passed. I was treated for laryngitis. When it began to happen more regularly, I went to a specialist. A round of steroids worked for a while. When the hoarseness returned, the doctor "scoped" my voice box. A three-foot, black, snake-like apparatus with a camera on the end of it was inserted down my nostril into my larynx, or voice box, in order to see my vocal cords. Once in position, I performed a series of "EEEEEEEEEE" sounds so my vocal cords could be recorded while vibrating, and analyzed. It wasn't fun.

Vocal cord polyps are the bane of the professional voice user. They're a common, yet rarely discussed, occupational hazard. People don't like to talk about them, lest they lose their jobs. Losing your "instrument" and your livelihood are real risks. So my diagnosis was distressing on many levels. Although I was under doctor's orders to stop talking *immediately,* practically, I had to tell my husband and boss. My husband's reaction was a lot like mine.

"You have to stop talking NOW?" he said. "This minute?"

It wasn't the diagnosis or the impending surgery that was most shocking: it was the imposed silence. It's an unusual prescription. Next, I called my boss, using the last of my reedy voice. He said the things you'd expect him to: not to worry about work and to get well soon; however, I wasn't convinced it was going to be okay jobwise.

After that call, another hurdle: My husband and I were throwing a party the next night for two dozen friends. It had been on the calendar a month. We were trying to figure out if we should cancel it, and I was writing on a yellow pad and my hand was getting tired. Then I had an "aha" moment. I raced into the boys' room and grabbed the "Fisher-Price Doodle Pro," an erasable writing board in their pile of toys. It was about 6 inches long and 5 inches wide with a pen dangling from its side and a bar you would slide on the top when you wanted to erase what you'd written. There was just enough room to write a few words at a time. It was similar to an Etch-A-Sketch but designed for kids. It was a terrific way to communicate and from that moment on I relied upon it for all face-to-face interaction. We went ahead with the party. My erasable board ended up being my favorite party favor ever. It was a memorable event.

But I couldn't use the board to communicate with my toddlers, ages one and two, because they couldn't read yet. So, I began to get creative. I snapped my fingers whenever my two-year-old son, Grey, called for me. He followed the sound to find me, à la pied piper. We also communicated though charades. It worked.

The most stressful moments happened outside the apartment. I remember trying to walk my dog, a pug named Milo, at the same time I had Grey with me. When it was time to go inside again, Grey didn't want to and dug his heels in. I shook my head no but couldn't verbally communicate why we needed to go inside. He wasn't happy and broke into tears.

It was also dangerous to take Grey to the zoo or other crowded places during that time. When he was excited by something and tried to wander away, I felt panic not being able to call out to him. He'd look up at me, his big brown eyes full of incomprehension. After a few tries, I gave up taking him out alone until I'd recovered.

But by far, my silence was hardest on my husband. He's the strong silent type. I'm the talkative one. He reluctantly took up the yoke of conversation initiator. He struggled with forced monologues and sharing his streams of consciousness. It was amusing for me, but I felt sorry for him. He was out of his element and missed my voice.

Meanwhile, I began to enjoy a newfound Zen. I realized how calm I felt. Without being able to speak, I was keeping my own counsel for the first time in my life. I wasn't asking other people for their opinions. I wasn't asking for assistance. I was just being with myself. I was also listening like never before.

New Yorkers were never nicer. During my time of silence, almost everyone was polite and patient with me. Some people assumed I was deaf or impaired as well, and spoke V-E-R-Y L-O-U-D-L-Y or sloooowly. Others thought I was a foreigner. But either way, they were drawn to my calm presence. I was nonthreatening and nonjudgmental, and as a result of my stellar listening skills, quite popular. People took the opportunity to talk to me about all kinds of personal things.

The surgery took place the morning ABC News Anchor Peter Jennings died. He was my favorite anchorman and a professional role model. As I sat in my wheelchair in the pre-op waiting room of Mount Sinai in my surgical garb and paper bracelet, I watched the news of his passing and prayed it wasn't an omen. I worried that my voice wouldn't be the same and that my career would be over.

Fortunately, my surgery was a success. My voice was restored, and I did return to work the following month.

Now, years later, I look back at my month of silence as a kind of unexpected spiritual retreat. It was enlightening. I now understand the value of silence and how, for monks in Tibet and other practitioners of silent meditation, it can truly change a person. I also know that it can be experienced right here, in the middle of New York City, with millions of people around. The problem is I don't practice it enough. I feel certain I could regain some of that inner peace by speaking less and listening more. The challenge now is doing it.

Fur

I t was already dead when I bought it," I sheepishly say as I bid good morning to the elevator man who has just complimented me on my fur coat. I feel the need to explain away my guilt for owning not one, not two, not three, not four, but five fur coats – not to mention fur jackets, vests, hats, handbags and scarves.

I feel like Cruella de Vil just writing this. But they *are* dead long before I fall in love with the incredible softness of the pelts, the instant chic, and glamorous styling. I feel elegant and successful wearing a fur coat. My kids hug me longer, rubbing their cheeks against me while snuggling into the softness with an abandon that my wool, cashmere and down coats never inspire.

But I get that it's not politically correct. I'm appalled and mortified by the very thought of images I've seen of baby seals, with their innocent and huge eyes, being bludgeoned to death. Even photos of minks raised in captivity make me want to avert my eyes. Despite those feelings, however, when I walk into a store and see a gorgeous piece, I still think to myself, "Would *my* not buying this item, actually stop it from happening? That's the issue. I don't really believe I'm part of the problem.

Fur is lightweight and warm. That's not an easy combination to find. For someone who deals with winter, it's a way to rationalize the purchase. That's about the only defense I can muster.

15

I will say I've loved animals my entire life. I've never lived without a dog or cat for more than a respectable mourning period. I treasure them dearly, so the fur issue is a quandary. The very thought of all the precious fur I've petted on my living, breathing darlings is enough to give me pause. Shedding fur is something I'm no stranger to either: I have sticky rollers to lift it off clothes, as well as vacuums at the ready.

Moreover, I've now spent literally tens of thousands of dollars on vets and animal hospitals, sparing no expense when it came to treating my dogs' illnesses. These have included: diabetes, pancreatitis, and epilepsy for Milo the pug, and a total hip replacement and knee surgery for Toby the Cavalier King Charles Spaniel. I've taxed my marriage by never giving up and insisting we pay for whatever is fixable.

Without so much as a single class in veterinary medicine, my passion for my pets has found my husband Rob and me dealing with emergency triage situations of life and death, where perhaps lesser-committed animal parents would have put them down. We've personally administered Valium rectally to stop seizure clusters, tested blood glucose levels, injected insulin regularly, and given hundreds of pills – all for the love of our furry family members. At one point in our lives, I administered two shots and sixteen pills a day, for four years to my diabetic and epileptic pug Milo. Good thing I had stopped working the year he contracted his diseases! My days revolved around his medicine schedule. Managing my two human babies at the same time was a piece of cake compared to tending to Milo's needs.

"But Amanda, he's a *dog*," my husband Rob pointed out in the face of mounting and staggering health costs for Milo's month of intravenous feeding and round-the-clock nursing in the intensive care unit at the Animal Medical Center in New York City, for a case of acute pancreatitis.

"I know he's a dog, but he's my dog, and he was mine before I met you," I pleaded. "And he can get better. It's not like he has terminal cancer. "

Rob loved Milo too, but he's a reasonable person and the bills were unbelievable. Of course, we paid them and many more during Milo's life span. We saw Milo to the bitter end; he passed away at age thirteen. Afterwards, Rob understandably made me promise there would be no extraordinary measures taken whenever a new dog became ill. Fast-forward half a year when our six-month-old Cavalier King Charles puppy, named Toby, was diagnosed with multiple bone deformities requiring an immediate hip replacement and knee surgery. With my promise to Rob at the forefront of my mind, I listened to the diagnosis and replied to the top animal hip replacement surgeon in the country: "Let's schedule it." Poor Rob! There I went again! When it comes to Toby, there's also the issue of his staggering hair care, which costs more than mine does. Grooming that dog's fur is non-stop. He's high maintenance.

But that's not where my furry activities end. There's also charity: I've volunteered at animal shelters, donated to local ASPCAs, and raised money for a visitation room at the Animal Medical Center in memory of Milo. So how to reconcile my fur wardrobe? It really is a very hairy, or rather furry, matter.

Postscript: Shortly after this piece was written, I realized I <u>was</u> part of the problem and stopped purchasing real fur.

A Curious Case

One night when I was very young, perhaps five or six years old, I woke up with my right foot, and a good deal of my right leg, stuck under my bedroom door. The door led from the room I shared with my sister, Allison, into the hallway of our Mediterranean-style home in the Northern California suburb of Hillsborough. It was a regular-sized, white-painted door, which opened the normal way, swinging out from left to right from inside our bedroom into the hallway, barely touching the rosy pink, shag wall-to-wall carpet beneath it. The door always glided smoothly over that carpet. I would guess there was the normal space in between; nothing more, nothing less. It certainly wasn't new carpeting or a new door.

I was thin-boned and prone to sleep walking. I made regular nocturnal visits to my nanny Petra's bedroom downstairs off the kitchen, so it wasn't usual for me to be on the go at night. What *was* unusual was waking up stuck under the door. I remember trying to move but couldn't. I was sitting on the floor in my pink frilly nightgown with one leg stuck beneath the door, practically to my knee. At first, I thought I was dreaming. Then, when I realized I was awake, I felt a rising panic; I was getting hot and my breath was jagged from exertion as I tried to pull my foot and leg out from underneath the wood.

"Allison!" I called to my sister who was across our room sleeping soundly in her matching white-eyelet canopy bed. "Help! Help! Wake up!" I was beginning to cry.

After what seemed like an eternity, Allison did wake up. She was three years older than I.

"Okay, Okay,'" she sleepily called back, as she trudged toward me. She turned on the overhead light switch near the door, looked down and started reaching for the door handle to open the door *with me* underneath it! "I'll get mom and dad," she was saying. It was literally a slow-motion nightmare.

"No, stop, stop! Don't use this door!" I screamed. Now I was *really* panicked. Her eyes widened as she got my message. She couldn't move the door without moving me. Immediately, she redirected herself and used the other door out of our bedroom, which led to our bathroom and out into the hallway. I could hear her yelling for our parents as she ran down the hall to their bedroom.

The next thing I remember is my dad, my mom, Petra and Allison all staring down at me, their mouths agape. Then there was a discussion about how this could have happened and how to fix it. Meantime, I remember thinking: *They don't know what to do! What if they need to cut my leg off?* I started sobbing harder, and cried, "Please get me out of here!" I was scared and imagined the worst. I pictured myself showing up at school without a leg. No more running. *Crutches forever.* My jagged breaths and mounting panic made me inadvertently move my leg, making it hurt even more. The compression between the floor and door were already cutting into it. My foot began to feel numb. By far, though, the worst part was psychological: it looked freaky. From my vantage point, my skinny white leg literally ended beneath the door and my right foot had disappeared.

My dad, who was coincidentally an orthopedic surgeon, was standing there in his dark green bathrobe, scratching his head. Then, he calmly crouched down to my level and began to try to free me, by slowly and gently attempting to rotate my leg a bit here and there, gingerly endeavoring to coax it from the gap. When I winced, he'd stop before trying it again. It didn't work.

Looking back, it really was a mystery – a very curious incident. I must have been sleep walking when it happened. For a time, Allison and Petra joined me on the floor, talking to me and holding my hands.

In the end, the decision was made to cut the carpet out from under my leg. My dad began using scissors and knives to get the job done. I worried he might cut me by mistake. I turned my head away and stopped looking at the blades. I was getting very cold by that point and my backside ached from sitting in such an awkward position for so long. My dad paused as I carefully lay flat on the carpet, staring at the ceiling. My dad worked methodically, to cut and lift away the carpet from the bare floor beneath my leg, creating space. Then he inched my leg out horizontally to the side very slowly until it cleared the door. Suddenly, I was free.

I looked at my leg, still attached to my body, as though I'd never seen it before. All I wanted to do was touch it. I remember rubbing my hand all the way from my knee down to my foot and back again. I had a dent in the skin for a bit – proof that the ordeal had been real. I don't remember how long the holes in the carpet remained. I wish I'd kept a piece of it or that someone had taken a photo. In the end, my foot and leg escaped their bondage unscathed. For me, though, the curious incident remains a great mystery forever trapped in my memory.

Look At It This Way

"Remember, every decision you make is a mistake." I'll never forget my father telling me that. It was just one of his verbal gems. He was an original thinker, to say the least. He was full of eccentric advice, which he gladly shared. "What does that mean?" was my constant retort. He spoke to me as an adult from the time I was a kid. The problem was, I really didn't understand the irony of a lot of the advice. "It means, don't worry about it," he replied, shrugging his shoulders and laughing with his eyes. Dad always had what I think of as an "existential shrug," which he employed to emphasize the folly of it all.

"It don't make no never mind," was his favorite saying. "No communal TV," was another mantra. He believed everyone should have his or her own TV in our house, and control of the remote. A corollary was his maxim: "No family room." When I was in junior high and had to choose between chemistry and physics, he said, "Take them both, of course! That's what every kid does in Japan." He wasn't kidding. He was a bit tone deaf when it came to the state of my psyche. I was a worrier and his advice rarely took that into account. His advice was unfiltered – it didn't depend on his audience. He always advocated the road less taken. He was disappointed when I chose to go to law school and passed up a chance to work in trade publishing in Hong Kong. I was scared and chose the safer route. It didn't take me long to realize my mistake. Fast-forward a few years, when I left my mind-numbing job with a prestigious law firm to pursue a career in television news. Dad was ecstatic and set a fancy lunch date. "Everyone should quit a job once in his or her life. It's the greatest feeling in the world!" he said gleefully, as we sat together in the dining room of the St. Francis Hotel in San Francisco.

Dad wasn't a practical man, but he was a brilliant one. A fine artist who also illustrated medical books, an orthopedic surgeon, an avid reader who studied the Times Literary Supplement like a bible, an MBA graduate later in life for interest, a collector of kinetic art, a jazz lover, a baseball fan, and a man who loved to travel.

When it came to travel, he believed no one should ever check luggage. For years we all tried, but eventually everyone but him gave up. He'd still spend hours editing his wardrobe to fit in his carry-on bag. Once he bought me a small suede satchel with a travel set inside, which included a tiny cut crystal bottle filled with laundry soap, a thin, 6-foot clothesline and a set of miniature clothes clips. He was a man who delighted in the extraordinary.

And he too, could be extraordinary. Once when he was on call for the local emergency room, he saved a man whose arm was caught in a garbage truck. Others were going to cut the arm off; dad had the *truck* taken apart. When our cat developed epilepsy dad treated him with human prescription drugs, and he lived to 21. When my sister developed a potentially blinding eye problem in college, dad started her on a controversial vitamin C therapy that worked. As an older man, he volunteered several times aboard a medical Mercy Ship anchored off the coast of Liberia where he performed surgeries for several months at a time for those in need.

He was a proud Canadian, an old-fashioned gentleman and quite dapper. He wore bow ties and jackets, caps and suspenders. But his conservative exterior belied his odd, original personality. With me tagging along, he would often wander into a store, nod hello to the shopkeeper then nonchalantly walk into the backroom. "Where are we going, Dad?" I'd ask in a hushed voice, trying to look natural. "Just follow me," he'd say. In the back, he kept his own stash of books, records, or whatever it was they sold, on hold. He was constantly adding to his collections. These excursions were always followed by a meal, usually at some obscure restaurant he'd recently read about. There, he'd regale me with facts and stories, frequently asking me rhetorically, *"Remember that?"* despite the fact that I usually hadn't been born yet. He had a photographic memory and encyclopedia-like knowledge, coupled with grand ideas about life that he loved to share. For example, he'd tell you places to go, the best hotels, the best art, the best sports -- even the importance of eating mustard on hotdogs. He could not, for the life of him, understand how I could hate mustard. That conversation always ended in the good-natured, 'I give up' "shrug." Once, he told me I had an "arrested development" because for years I missed a difficult old boyfriend when I had a really nice new one. "You want the frog, when you have the prince," he said. Truer words were never spoken.

As an adult, I once asked him for a book recommendation. David Foster Wallace's *Infinite Jest* was his pick. I tried in earnest to read it many times before giving up in frustration. He could have chosen something easier for me to share with him, but he was clueless that way. I'm sure it never occurred to him, and I was too proud to tell him. He was a kind person. He told my mom, my sister and me that we were beautiful - too often for anyone to believe him. He had zero credibility after a while on that front, but I loved him for it. He always told me, "When I die, I want my tombstone to read, "Ned Grove is dead. Don't worry about it'." Oh Dad, I won't ... but I miss you.

Banned

You can't come to closing arguments. Your mom doesn't want you there."

Deborah, my mom's senior law associate sounded stressed. It was 6:00 am on the morning of the final day of the court case, when both sides present their summaries to the jury. My mom was the defense attorney litigating the case.

"What do you mean I can't come?" I asked, feeling a rush of shock and dismay. She'd woken me up and I still didn't fully understand what she'd said. I'd been observing the trial in court all week. More than that, I'd been an unofficial part of my mom's trial team. I'd been watching the case and taking notes, then meeting with my mom and Deborah each afternoon to debrief and go over my comments.

"She just called me in a panic and told me to tell you that you're not allowed to come this morning. I'm sorry Amanda."

"Why?" I sounded like the hurt child I was.

"She said you'll make her nervous and she doesn't want you there. She's afraid she'll lose."

"That's ridiculous! I cried. "Why didn't she call me herself?"

"I don't know. She told me to do it. I'm really sorry Amanda."

"I don't understand this, but I can't just walk in there now, can I?"

"No, I'm afraid you can't. I don't get it either but there's nothing we can do. Sorry, I have to go."

I took a deep breath, holding back tears.

"Ok, Deborah. I understand. Good luck."

"Thanks, Amanda."

I'd known Deborah for several years by that point. She was about 15 years older than I was. She was smart and friendly. She'd worked with my mom for a long time. She genuinely sounded sympathetic, but she was just the messenger and didn't have the authority to override my mom's decision.

I hung up feeling deeply stung and distraught. I was sitting in my apartment in the Marina District of San Francisco. I was a third-year law student at the University of California Hastings College of the Law. I had just finished final exams and was on spring break, which just happened to coincide with a trial my mom was litigating in court downtown. After all the years of her being a lawyer, it was my first time actually being able to see her in court.

I was eight years old when she went to law school. I was now in my mid-twenties. She'd had a long and successful career as a lawyer by this time. She was a partner at a San Francisco law firm. She specialized in insurance defense, litigating medical malpractice claims (essentially defending doctors). The week before this case began, my mom was talking about her upcoming trial and I was talking about my school break with nothing planned. I asked her if I could come to court and watch for a day. She agreed.

I was excited when I arrived at the courthouse the first morning. I took a seat in the back and just soaked it all in. It was great to see my mom in her arena. She was wonderful – she had a large persona and commanding presence. She was theatrical, but instilled confidence. She spoke clearly and passionately. I felt a lot of pride. It was a thrill to finally see her in action. After the first day, my mom came over and asked for my opinions, observations and thoughts. I had many. By this time, I was quite knowledgeable and had observed many other courtroom cases. I was another pair of educated eyes and ears in the courtroom. My mom was very interested in what I had to say, and welcomed my suggestions. She asked me to come back to her office and discuss them. Then she asked me to come to court every day and take notes, and to share them with her and Deborah afterwards. I agreed. It was a wonderful week.

I loved being included and sharing strategy. I felt important and valued. It was a special time for me, as a law student, to share this experience with my mother, a trial lawyer. I immersed myself in the case. I felt like a very welcome addition. Or at least I had, until this morning. This call had arrived without warning, leaving me shocked and insulted.

It wasn't just being banned from the courtroom after feeling like an "insider" that hurt me so deeply. It was also the fact that my mom didn't call me herself to explain. She'd added insult to injury by having poor Deborah deliver the news. It was embarrassing. And what could I do now? Was I going to call my mom and plead with her at a time when she would be preparing for her closing argument that morning? If I called and upset her, then I would get blamed if the case didn't go well. She was obviously in a state of anxiety as it was. So, there I sat: angry, sad, embarrassed, mute, and impotent. It was a no win for me. Her not wanting me there crushed my spirit. But rather than just feeling *that* pain, as I sat there that morning, I was also questioning whether I had a *right* to feel that way. I tried to intellectualize the pain away: she was trying a case, it was her job, and anything that added stress should be removed. Maybe it wasn't personal? But how could it not be? Was I too thin-skinned?

I thought of all the years I'd missed spending time with her as she focused on her law career. She'd won many cases in her day. And yet, she lacked the confidence to have me watch her finish a case. Why? I had always supported her. I'd never criticized her. I was becoming a lawyer in large part because of her. Whether she won or lost made no difference to how I would regard her or my love for her. Yet here I was: banned from the courtroom. I pitied her for her lack of self-esteem.

The next time I saw her, she told me she'd won the case. She was smiling and light about it.

"Congratulations," I said with false enthusiasm. Then I asked her, "Why wasn't I allowed to come to closing arguments? It hurt my feelings."

She just laughed and dismissed me with a wave of her hand.

"Oh, it was better for me that way," she replied.

It was clear we weren't going to discuss it further. I left it there. What was there to say? I never asked to watch her in court again and she never offered. She continued to bask in the glory of her "brilliant career" for years to come. I'd listen to her tell other people about it. Inside, though, I felt a tough nut of resentment. I knew the truth.

Aunt Ruth

S he lay motionless in bed. She was in the late stage of pancreatic cancer. I sat beside her full of grief. My aunt was 67. She'd retired from her job as a foreign correspondent just two years before. She'd lived most of her adult life as a journalist in Asia, but moved to California upon retirement. It was supposed to be a temporary home for her and her two Siamese cats. She hated the cold Northern California weather -- so different from the balmy breezes of Singapore. She disliked living in a retirement community after the exotic abodes of her prior life. She'd struggled to find her self-esteem in retirement. She'd begun tutoring a high school student near Berkeley. She'd been dating a loser who lived in the complex just to break the monotony, before he went back to his girlfriend. She'd barely unpacked since she'd moved there. She was drowning her sorrows watching television and eating ice cream. In short, she'd been depressed. Now, she was dying.

Growing up, Aunt Ruth had always been my most colorful relative. My mom's only sister, six years her junior, Aunt Ruth had always pooh-poohed tradition. She grew up in New Jersey and fought convention every step of the way. I loved her stories: how she wouldn't marry the nice, boring man who proposed in her 20s, even though her parents begged her to; how she left quiet Northwestern University in the 60s to enroll and protest at the University of Michigan; how her first job in journalism was working for a newspaper in Hawaii. There she met her first husband, who was also a journalist but looked like a gorgeous surfer. That job led to thirty years working as a bureau chief for UPI and later for DPA, in posts including Beijing, Tokyo, Boston, Malaysia, and Singapore. She'd regale me with stories of covering events, including the America's Cup in Australia and interviewing Malcolm Forbes and Elizabeth Taylor on his yacht. But the most memorable tales were of her love life: by the end, she'd had three husbands and countless romances. Endlessly driven, adventure seeking, and childless (she'd had a miscarriage during her second marriage), she'd lived life on her own terms, with a childlike enthusiasm and wonder. She was unconventional and unapologetic. One example: On a trip to New Zealand in her forties, she visited a sheep station on a group tour. The tour guide was the owner, whom she found very attractive. He asked her why she was leaving as she boarded the bus. That was it. She never got on the bus! That romance led to an engagement at one time, but the distance from New Zealand to Tokyo proved too much. She really wasn't cut out to live on a sheep farm anyway. She was smart, funny, irreverent, and non-judgmental. When I asked for her advice, desperately uncertain the day before my first wedding, she advised me: "Say 'I do' and think 'for now,' that's what I always do."

All my life, I'd call her wherever she was working in the world, just to hear her say, "Hi Hon," in her a high-pitched, sing-songy voice. She was always up early, drinking coffee and writing her first story of the day. She was young at heart – in her attitude, dress and desires; yet her mood was often unsteady: sometimes excited and optimistic; other times, depressed and pessimistic. She worried about finding her next love, the stock market, losing her job, and growing old. As an adult, we traveled together to far-away lands like Bali, Morocco, and Istanbul. She made me feel together, confident and wise. I always planned our trips. Somehow, despite our ages, I often felt like the adult. She asked for my opinion and counsel as much or more so than I asked for hers. She needed reassurance, which I always gave. In return, I needed to feel loved and special, which she made me feel. Over the years, on camels, in desert windstorms, in souks and in hot air balloons, we bonded again and again. We made each other feel better in the world. I felt stronger and braver around her. We liked who we were in each other's eyes. We called ourselves, "The Intrepid."

She was always my wingman, literally and figuratively, despite the distances and the infrequent visits. On my first trip to Disneyland when I was very young, we went on a two-person rocket-type ride. Everyone else's rocket was rising higher while circling, but I couldn't figure out the simple control. She was my copilot and sat behind me, as adults were required to do. The whole ride went by with us making the same endless circles below.

"I can't do it," I cried out to her in frustration. Although she tried to assist, the ride ended too soon. I felt so stupid. Even my younger brother made his rocket rise.

We were the losers! She just laughed. She didn't mind, and I loved her for it.

Many years later, she wanted to take my kids to Disney World in Florida for their first time. When the boys started crying on the Haunted House ride, she was truly perplexed. "What's wrong with them?" she asked. "They're only five and six!" I exclaimed, defending their poor form and my poor judgment. I'd forgotten how scary it could be. Later that trip, as we walked through the hotel lobby, she offered to watch the boys while I went into the gift shop. When I returned, I found the boys with a hotel clerk and my aunt across the room playing a slot machine. She'd outsourced the babysitting! It was hard to stay mad at Aunt Ruth though -- she was so childlike herself. It was part of her unique charm; she was endearing that way. I worried more about losing her at Disney World than my boys. She would simply wander off and I'd be left holding onto the boys' hands scanning the crowd. Frequently, she'd appear having purchased yet another Disney-themed t-shirt for herself. Her wardrobe reflected a serious lack of style and age-appropriate convention. Comfort was key. Sneakers were her preferred footwear. She even liked to travel with disposable underwear. Her hair looked best blond, but often was a strange bronze color. She said it was difficult for Asians colorists to get blond right. Maybe so, but she didn't try hard enough. These quirks were hard to reconcile with another side of her that would spare little expense when it came to fine jewelry and, in later years, facelifts.

Now, lying in bed, that youthful face was ravaged by disease. Her hair was snow white. Her once beautiful body was emaciated. Half of the intrepid was setting sail forever.

Mr. Chang and Me

I saw him out of the corner of my eye. Perfect face, perfect body. He was exactly right, and I wanted him. I hadn't seen anyone who stopped me in my tracks like that for years. And suddenly, here he was just a few blocks from my home and moving fast – too fast.

"Wait! Please," I called out. It's so uncomfortable to stop someone on the street in New York, but in this case it was necessary. Urgent. He did stop, but only when the woman he was with heard my call. I looked only at him, barely noticing her.

"He's perfect," I said, taking in every detail.

"Thanks," she said. I looked at her then. She was fair, tall and willowy.

"Where did you find him?" I asked. She seemed hesitant to say, but did. I was too dazzled by his Hollywood looks to absorb it.

"Can you stay right here for just a moment, please? I want my husband to meet him. He's just inside the shop next door. I'll run and get him."

"Okay," she said, sensing my urgency.

I dragged Rob out of the shop to meet my Mr. Right. He turned out to be named Mr. Chang, and was a much younger male. In fact, Mr. Chang was less than a year old. He was the perfect pug. Fawn-colored with an ink-black face, glossy fur and large, sparkling, root beer-colored brown eyes. I hadn't been able to even entertain the idea of bringing another pug into my life prior to meeting him that day. Four years earlier, my pug, Milo, had died. Two years after that we got Toby, a darling King Charles Cavalier Spaniel. He didn't remind me of Milo. He was something altogether different. He was a wonderful dog and yet, for the first time I felt the "pug tug" again.

Rob met Mr. Chang on the street that day but didn't warm to the idea of getting a second dog. He did acknowledge that Mr. Chang was a beauty, but that's where the conversation ended. I accepted defeat. Mr. Chang went down in my life history as the first pug since Milo to move me.

Several years passed before I saw Mr. Chang and his mom on the street again. It happened the same way: I saw an outstanding pug that stopped me in my tracks, then looked up the leash only to find the same woman smiling down at me. Only twice in four years had I ever stopped in awe of a pug and both times it was the one and only Mr. Chang. What were the odds? His mom and I chatted.

"I remember you! Did you end up getting a pug of your own?" she asked.

"Not yet," I said. "I'm still working on my husband." That night, I mentioned the coincidence of seeing Mr. Chang again to Rob, as well as my desire to get one like him. His response was more pugnacious this time. Why did I want another dog? Why wasn't one enough? He argued it was too expensive, too time-consuming, and just too much. I understood his points intellectually. Emotionally, though, for me *more* has always been better. I felt guilty though about Toby not being enough for me; however, I had also wanted another *human* baby when I already had one. Was it that different? Of course, I loved Toby and that wouldn't change, but I still wanted to add a baby pug. I dropped the issue again. I resolved to spend more time with Toby.

One summer night in Southampton, New York in 2018, I took Toby for a walk a little later than usual. Just as I was rounding my block, I saw a glorious pug. My heart leapt. I looked up and there once again was the same woman! What were the odds?!

"Mr. Chang!" I shouted with glee from across the street. "I can't believe it. Every time I see a pug I like, it's always you. I promise I'm not stalking you."

This time, Mr. Chang was with both his mom and his dad. It turns out they had just bought the house for sale around the corner from ours. I was overjoyed and immediately suggested we walk to my house so I could once again attempt to convince Rob that it was time to add a pug to our family. Mr. Chang's parents were more than happy to assist. I was so excited and nervous I chatted non-stop. This was fate! This was going to be the turning point. When we got to the house, I opened the gate and we let Mr. Chang run free and meet Toby on the lawn. It was a joyous homecoming. Rob, as well as our sons Grey and Ford all reacted happily to the impromptu gathering, and we proceeded to have drinks as the afternoon sun set. Mr. Chang made himself at home, chewing one of Toby's dog bones and nestling between my husband and younger son, Ford, on the outdoor sofa. From time to time, Mr. Chang and Toby would enter the house for water. They were getting along. Joy! My heart pounded in my chest. I willed Rob to see what I saw and feel the same way about it. I drank too much wine in an effort to calm my nerves. My eyes darted back and forth watching the scene. I felt elated, jubilant. I could not believe <u>he</u> was here. I felt like I was entertaining royalty – I could not do enough for Mr. Chang. I let him run free in my house, something no other visiting dog has ever done. Mr. Chang's parents were fun too, and we made plans to see them again. Afterwards, though, Rob said he *still* didn't want another dog.

"One dog at a time," he said.

I remain undeterred. It was serendipity to run into my pug "crush" three times in four years. Fate is obviously bringing Mr. Chang and me together. He's now my neighbor. Rob can continue to protest, but it's only a matter of time. As the poet Emily Dickinson wrote, "The heart wants what the heart wants."

Postscript: In January of 2021, Pia - a baby pug - joined our family. Pia, Toby, and Mr. Chang are now neighbors and friends.

Ten Minutes and Eighteen Years

*T*he gothic-style reception hall is filled with high school applicants and their parents waiting for their admission appointments. My 13-year-old son, Ford, and I have just driven two and a half hours through morning traffic to this bucolic boarding school. We've never been here before.

At least we're on time, and Ford's new blue blazer fits him well, I'm thinking to myself as we walk through the arched stone entryway, Ford two steps ahead. I glance around the imposing room. I see the check-in table, as well as a wall of tapestries on the left and a high, beamed ceiling overhead. As I look to the right, I see a row of stain glass windows, and a man staring at me. *Really staring*. This isn't a casual glance. It feels urgent. He's also *smiling* in a frozen, strained way. A woman stands beside him reading a pamphlet, oblivious.

How strange! I think to myself. *And so inappropriate to stare at me that way in front of his wife. He's not even blinking.*

I give him a quick, quizzical smile just so he won't think I'm rude, then look away. I try to shake it off and focus on the receptionist sitting behind the desk.

"Good morning," I say brightly, "This is Ford Holmén and I'm his mom, Amanda. We're here for his 11:20 tour and interview."

"Welcome," she says smiling. "Please make yourself comfortable and we'll be right with you."

Just as we move away from the desk, I hear my name.

"Amanda!"

I turn and it's him again, moving towards us. My mind is now working overtime. *How do I know this man?* My mind rolodexes through my mental card catalog: is he a parent at another school, someone I used to work with? He *does* look familiar. He's tall and solidly built, with a full beard.

I brace myself. Although there are at least a dozen other people in the room, I'm not aware of any of them. I'm completely focused on his face.

"Hi," I say, smiling wanly up at him, as I stall for time. I feel stressed that I have no idea who he is, while he so obviously knows me. I decide to use an age-old tactic of getting the person whose name you can't recall to say his or her name first by introducing that person to someone else. I turn towards Ford.

"This is my son, Ford," I say, gesturing with my left hand before using it to usher Ford forward to meet him.

"Hi Ford," he says shaking Ford's outstretched hand. "I'm Elliot."

Elliot! I feel a shock wave rock my body. It's my ex-husband, whom I haven't seen in eighteen years. In a split second, I go from feeling disoriented, to giddy, to mortified I didn't recognize him. I start rationalizing: *It's hard to recognize someone with a beard! He's also gained some weight. He was always so thin!*

After processing his looks, I start thinking of *mine*. I hope I look good. Does this cardigan make me look fat? I wish I'd taken it off before I walked in. Thank goodness my hair is down, but I wish I'd washed it this morning.

"Hi Amanda," he repeats, breaking my chain of thought.

"Oh, my gosh, Elliot, it's so good to see you," I look into his eyes. Now I'm the one holding the stare. It *is* so good to see him! I've always liked Elliot. I liked him very, very much. I even loved him. But I didn't *love* him enough to stay married to him. That was the problem.

We'd met in law school in California when he was in his third year and I was in my first. We married after I graduated. I was twenty-five. I knew I wasn't ready to get married but went through with it anyway because I didn't have the guts to stop it. I tried to call it off once, a few months before the wedding, but Elliot convinced me it was nerves. Even my own family dismissed my concerns because they loved him. No one wanted to hear it. My mom and sister told me everyone was looking for someone like him and if I didn't marry him, I'd regret it for the rest of my life. Just relax, they said, I was doing the right thing. So, I ignored my feelings and went with it. After all, I told myself, he was my best friend and I loved him.

After the wedding, we lived in San Francisco for four years before moving to New York City to pursue our careers. All the while, I was restless and unhappy. I didn't like practicing law or being married. I felt stuck. I didn't want to settle down and have a family like Elliot did. I wanted to be free. I kept coming up with excuses for why I didn't want to move to the suburbs like many of his friends and their wives. After eight years, I finally gathered my courage and pulled the plug on our marriage. I hurt Elliot terribly and upset both our families. It was a hard blow for everyone. It felt like a death in the family. My grandmother told me she felt ashamed and embarrassed by my actions. Everyone loved Elliot and his family. *After all these years, I still felt guilty about all the pain I'd caused.*

After our divorce I wished we could have remained friends, but as we never had children to bind us it was easier to just let go. We communicated very rarely. He called to tell me he was getting remarried; I did the same a year later. When he had his first baby, I sent a gift. He followed suit when my first son was born. That was it, until just six months before this unexpected boarding school encounter, when Elliot learned my father had died (a year after the fact) and wrote me a text of condolence. We'd caught up a bit on each other's lives in that exchange. Still, I hadn't *seen* him in almost two decades.

Now here we were, face to face. And his wife was here too. She joined him now looking pensive. She was tall like him and swathed in an orange scarf and long, russet peasant skirt. She had long, wavy, slightly unnaturally colored orange-auburn hair, which flowed down her shoulders. It was an interesting, earth mother type ensemble. She was attractive. Elliot introduced us and I reached out eagerly to shake her hand. I was nervous and excited to meet her.

"It's *so* great to finally meet you, Laura. I feel like I know you."

I'd always felt a debt of gratitude to this woman whom he loved and had built a happy life with. She alleviated some of the guilt I felt about our divorce.

"I have to give you a hug!" I hear myself saying next, as I inexplicably draw her close into a brief and awkward embrace. When we part, she looks a bit perplexed.

I'm aware of an uncomfortable silence as we all continue to stare at each other. I search for something to say to keep the conversation going. I recall some of the things Elliot shared with me in his text and follow up on them now in rapid succession.

"I thought all your sons went to school in Brooklyn?" I ask, genuinely confused as to why they are looking at this boarding school in Connecticut.

Elliot explained they owned a weekend house nearby and were exploring.

"This is our first boarding school interview ever," he said. Then: "I can't believe we've run into each other here, when we've *never* run into each other in the city."

Something about the heightened emphasis of the word "never" made me realize he was nervous too. Maybe he was explaining that for his wife's benefit?

"Where do you live?" Laura suddenly interjected, looking at me intently.

"The Upper East Side," I said, meeting her gaze.

"We live in Tribeca," she said.

I nod and smile as though it's the most interesting thing I've ever heard. Again, there's a lull in the conversation. Elliot is just standing there. Hoping to ease the tension, I begin talking animatedly about my older son's boarding school experience at Deerfield, another boarding school. At the same time, I'm fumbling around in my purse to find my phone so I can show them pictures of him. When I stop talking to catch my breath, I hardly listen to what they say. My mind is racing. *I just cannot believe what's happening. Just standing here together is surreal!* My pulse is elevated. I feel flush.

While we continue to make small talk, on a deeper level the floodgates of memory are opening of our ten-year relationship. I feel desperate to hold onto the connection before it's lost.

"How was your father's 80th birthday?" I ask Elliot.

"Great," he said without much enthusiasm.

Now you've done it, I think to myself. Maybe he hadn't told his wife about texting me after he'd learned my dad died, and I'm getting him in trouble*? Too late now.* I forge ahead.

"Do you have any photos of your parents? I'd love to see them," I continued. "They're such great people!"

Just then, a tall young man with sandy-colored hair approached. It was their son, who had just finished his interview.

"This is Stanley, "Elliot said.

"Hi, Stanley. I'm Amanda," I said shaking his hand. "I'm an old friend of your Dad's. It's a pleasure to meet you." I meant it.

Then his son and my son introduced themselves and shook hands. It was a monumental moment for me. *In another life, these two boys might have been brothers*, I think to myself. Now here we were, everyone fine, no one childless. Elliot didn't hate me. I could tell. This unexpected reunion was a gift that life had bestowed upon me and I savored it. I felt something lift inside of me. *All was well.* Finally, I felt exonerated from the guilt of the divorce. I'd not been able to let go of it until now. The reconciliation had only taken ten minutes -- ten minutes and eighteen years.

"Excuse me, sorry to interrupt," an admissions' team member approached us sheepishly. "It's time for your interview." He looked directly at Elliot and Laura.

As they said their hasty goodbyes to Ford and me, I reached out and hugged them both again (who knew when nervous I became such a hugger?).

"It's been *so* lovely to see you both. Good luck." I beamed at them. I felt euphoric. It felt like a piece of me had returned and its homecoming was long overdue.

They hurried off. I felt sorry for Elliot. If his mind were in as much nostalgic turmoil as mine was at that moment, it would be difficult to interview well.

The receptionist interrupted my thoughts.

"You can't believe how many people run into each other here! It always amazes us." She shook her head up and down for emphasis.

"Yes, it really *is* a small world," I said, smiling back at her. We hadn't moved more than two yards from her desk since we'd arrived.

Then it was our turn to begin our tour and interview.

I said nothing to Ford about who he had just met, or why I spent so much time talking to him and his family. Ford didn't ask. I decided not to share the information. Years earlier, I'd told my boys that I'd been divorced. It was old history. Today was Ford's day. He was focused on the school, the tour and his interview. I was distracted; fortunately, Ford didn't seem to notice. As my body walked through classrooms, dorms, and athletic fields, my mind was lost in a contented fog, obsessing about the past and replaying the encounter. I realized that what I had wanted and needed all along was to feel *forgiven.* Forgiven by Elliot, yes, but *also by myself.* Now I did. We'd both found love again. Our children had met. It felt as if we'd walked across a bridge spanning two decades. It was healing. I briefly fantasized about the unlikely possibility that our sons might be friends at the school and maybe even room together.

After Elliot and his wife left for their interviews, I immediately texted my husband, Rob, about running into him after eighteen years. He replied "Wow." I couldn't wait to talk more about it, but I'd have to. We had a full day ahead at the school, as well as a long drive home. When Rob finally walked through the door after work later that night, I took his arm and led him into our bedroom.

"I can't wait to talk to you alone!" I said.

"About what?" He asked.

"What do you mean about *what*? About running into my ex-husband after eighteen years!" I respond, flabbergasted he had to ask.

"Oh, I totally forgot about that!" he said.

I rolled my eyes at him. I certainly hadn't married the jealous type.

The next day, I wrote Elliot a text. I told him how great it was to see him and to meet his wife and son. I apologized for not recognizing him with his full beard. I said his son was very handsome and reminded me of him. I wished them well. He responded that it felt like, "a wall had been breached." He apologized that he wasn't, "totally present or charming" because he wrote he was "flummoxed." He said he was glad we ran into each other.

Like I said, Elliot was always a good person. Now, finally, I felt like one too.

Bittersweet

*E*njoy your boys while they're young. They grow up so fast. It seems like yesterday when mine were little."

Wise words from mature women who looked at me with my two little boys in tow and saw themselves in years past.

Suddenly it seems I'm there too. I've arrived at that same point where I say the same thing to other moms with small children. Just tonight I'd written it for the very first time to a friend with grade-school twin girls.

"Enjoy Halloween tonight with your daughters. It goes so fast."

I'd felt an 'I-told-you-so moment' of flash back, with a veritable chorus of women's voices ringing in my ears.

My oldest son, Grey, has started boarding school. He's not here anymore. He's there. I'm not waking him up, or making his breakfast, or aware of his day-to-day thoughts. He's not lying on the floor cuddling with our dog, Toby. He's not running late and needs me to remind him not to forget things as he rushes out the door. He's not eating too little food or too much sugar, or is he? I can't say. He doesn't live here anymore.

Tonight is Halloween. I remember Grey in his very first costume, a pumpkin. It had a green stem cap and an orange body. I have a photo of him in it with me. I wore a matching orange sweater and held him in my arms. Fast forward a few years, and I'm taking him and his younger brother, Ford, to nursery school in their costumes for the annual parade. My youngest, Ford, was a pirate his first Halloween, complete with a hat, little toy sword and eye patch.

Together on Halloween, year after year, the boys gathered candies in plastic pumpkin buckets while I gathered memories of them together. This year, Ford and his friends were all too busy studying for their high school SSAT entrance exam to get together and trick or treat. Instead, Ford spent an hour with a five-year-old kindergartener named George who lives in our apartment building, taking him around trick or treating in an act of kindness. George seemed so young in his racecar driver costume, and so tiny next to Ford who sported a soccer jersey and shorts (barely a costume as he wears that jersey a lot anyway). I made them pose for a photo near the door of our apartment. I'd decorated the exterior of the door, as well as its threshold with fake graves, large spiders, a huge pumpkin, and an ugly witch. Neither my husband nor son thought it was necessary. But it was to me.

"Hey," I told my husband, Rob, "Ford is still living here, and kids are still coming to the door this Halloween. I don't want to stop celebrating these holidays just because our kids are growing up." I held firm.

I happen to have a great cache of Halloween décor. My sons' godmother, Janet, is our patron saint of Halloween. She just loves it and throws herself into decorating. Her children are much older, so when my kids were young, she would come over and decorate our apartment with me for our annual kids' Halloween party. She brought us the most amazing decorations, including wall portraits that change from faces to skulls, little creepy light-up towns for tabletops, and shadowy hangmen decals for windows.

For the first time in thirteen years, I don't have any decorations set up inside the apartment. There's no party either. It seemed ridiculous to go through all the trouble to decorate inside. I wasn't going to go that far when no one shared my enthusiasm.

What will I do next year if we don't have any kids at home? That's what I'm thinking about tonight. Ford will likely follow his brother and go to boarding school in the fall. I push the question aside and focus on filling the giant, orange Halloween candy bowl. Rob and I will take turns manning the door.

At least one boy is still home, I tell myself in an effort to cheer myself up. But Ford wants to go to boarding school next year too, so it's not working. *Don't think about it now, I tell myself. He's still here. Don't think about the future.*

I make a new plan. Tonight, I'm going to selfishly hug Ford longer than he wants me to. I'm also going to numb the bittersweet pain with a bit of Halloween candy.

Strictly Ballroom

We are standing in a mansion with gleaming hardwood floors and crystal chandeliers aglow. It's a winter evening and people are dressed in dark suits and elegant attire including cocktail dresses and long gowns. In the ballroom, several opera singers are performing. It's a Russian event being held in New York City by a group of investors looking for funding for Russian-made aircraft. A small ensemble of musicians accompanies the opera singers. It's a private concert for eighty guests.

My husband, Rob, and I are enjoying the spectacle. The guests are standing along three sides of the ballroom watching as the performers take turns singing arias. It's a treat to be here. The cocktail hour has just ended. I've had a vodka drink, some interesting Russian hors d'oeuvres, and met some of my husband's business acquaintances. I'm wearing a lady-like black cocktail dress, a black cropped, three-quarter sleeve jacket of Persian broadtail, and pointy-toe, black suede pumps with bows.

The portly tenor finishes his aria, and the small orchestra begins to play classical music. It's waltz music in the grand tradition. We could be in Vienna, Moscow, or even Versailles. Suddenly, the tenor's eyes meet mine and he's striding toward me. Within seconds he's taking my arm. Before I realize what's happening, he's leading me toward the center of the ballroom. I look at Rob wide-eyed. Rob smiles at me. Suddenly the music begins.

I feel terribly self-conscious. I don't know how to waltz. I've never been taught. I feel exposed. All eyes are upon us. I feel my feet reacting too late. I'm mortified when I step on his toes. I feel embarrassed and awkward and can't wait until it's over. In the meantime, I smile at him and try not to look at my feet. I pretend that I know how to do this, and that I'm doing it well. But I'm not. I don't know how.

When he finally escorts me back to my husband's side, he smiles broadly, bows gallantly and moves back to center stage. The singing continues and the moment has passed for everyone except me.

"I never want to feel that way again," I whisper to Rob immediately afterwards.

"What? You looked great out there," he said. I think we both knew that I did *not* look great out there.

"Humph," I replied, annoyed at myself and everyone else, especially my parents. "I can't believe I never had lessons when I was growing up." I felt unsophisticated and inferior in that moment, and I didn't like it.

That's when I vowed to begin taking ballroom dancing lessons. And not just me; others would be taking dancing lessons too. I was determined that ballroom dancing was going to be a part of my sons' education if it was the last thing I did. As a result, they endured several years of Barclay dance classes. I loved watching the taller girls with their white gloves and the shorter boys in their blue blazers and khakis. I adored listening to the sound of the snare drum and three-piece band. The entire "Norman Rockwell" scene delighted me. I never missed a class. I took photos and videos and told my boys how much I loved them for going. It warmed my heart knowing that no son of mine would ever say that he never learned to dance. They were good sports until they finally ran screaming for the hills and quit. I let them, as none of their friends wanted to continue either. My work was done.

As for *my* training, it began a week after my mortifying experience with the opera singer, with a package of six classes at Arthur Murray Dance Studio. That led to another series of classes. They were all group classes. Each student had a teacher for the time period, but the dance floor was communal. My teachers were fine for the most part, but one had a very long pinky nail. I imagined him snorting cocaine with it and it distracted me from my mission. Another teacher was much shorter than I am. The main problem, though, was that I didn't like being touched by strangers. Ballroom dancing was, and still feels, too intimate for my taste. Add to that, the Arthur Murray studio pressured me to keep buying expensive packages of classes. I didn't like it, and decided to stop.

A few months later, I found my new teacher at a Valentine's Day masked ball. I attended solo because my husband was out of town. Manuel was at the event with an older lady, as her escort. I was seated next to him. He was charming, handsome, my age, and an experienced dance teacher. I felt comfortable with him. We exchanged information and the next week I began taking private classes.

Fast forward three years and we are still at it. From time to time, we venture out to different venues. I like dancing at Lincoln Center outdoors in the summer, but generally dislike the dance events held at places that feel like upstate community centers. Once, when Manuel was busy, I went to a Friday night class at a local church basement where everyone rotates partners. I felt manhandled by the elderly men who spun me around roughly. I didn't like the feeling of being passed around. I came home depressed and determined to have Rob join me next time. I begged him, but our conversation was brief.

"I don't recall taking ballroom dancing was a condition of our getting married," Rob said defensively.

"I know, but you're forcing me to dance at these strange places with other men! I feel very uncomfortable. We need to evolve together," I said, exasperated.

"Take Manuel." Rob said laughing. That was the end of the conversation. I've never gone anywhere ballroom dancing without Manuel since.

When I do, on the rare occasion, dance with Rob at someone's wedding or a fancy party, he feels that his middle school cotillion dance classes were more than adequate preparation. While I admire his confidence, sadly his skills are not up to par with mine now. I have surpassed him in terms of technique. In addition, he does not share my enthusiasm. I'm hoping we end up at a nifty country club in our sunset years dancing together. In the meantime, I continue to work toward my goal of becoming a beautiful ballroom dancer. I'm proud to say that I now have the skills to make it through any unexpected waltz that happens to come my way.

Falling From Grace

W ho wrote this?"

Mrs. Jenkins, my third-grade teacher, is furious. The whole class is sitting on the floor in front of her. She's gathered us for an emergency meeting.

I look up and see Mrs. Jenkins displaying my work. It's a white piece of paper folded in half to form a card. On the outside is a beautiful bow drawn in red crayon. The ends of the bow each extend down a third of the card ending in a decorative curlicue. Beneath of bow, written in neat blue crayon are the words: Happy Birthday Jim!

I know what's coming next. My heart is pounding. I look around looking for an escape. I'm trapped.

Mrs. Jenkins opens the card and shows the class. In perfect penmanship, inside it reads in capital letters: YOU STINK!

Mrs. Jenkins is a nice lady in her 60s, with high-teased, bright, strawberry-blonde hair that she wears in a bouffant. She has a kind face and smiles a lot. She's taught at North Hillsborough Elementary School for ages. I believe I'm her favorite this year, her teacher's pet. Mrs. Jenkins always asks me to do special things for her. For example, to draw a pirate on a giant poster board that will be on display along with our thematic work about pirates for parents' night. She says I have artistic ability. I feel special in her class. I'm always courteous and participate. I readily assist her whenever she asks.

In our class, Mrs. Jenkins has a tradition when it comes to birthdays. Everyone writes the person a birthday card. Last week, it was Jim's birthday, but he was at home sick. Mrs. Jenkins told us she would be gathering all our cards and putting them in a big manila envelope that would be sent home to Jim. My two best friends and I don't like Jim. We think he's a loser and a nerd. During our in-class time to work on Jim's birthday cards, we hatch a devious plan. We make our cards look great on the outside but say mean things on the inside.

I remember the thrill of walking up to Mrs. Jenkins' desk and announcing that I'd finished my card. She looked at it and smiled.

"What a pretty card Amanda!" She said approvingly.

"Thanks Mrs. Jenkins," I said. I held my breath as, *without opening it*, she put it in the large manila envelope. I'd been nervous. Could I get away with this? I wasn't used to rule breaking or risk taking. This feeling was exciting and new. I walked back to my desk and smiled at my co-conspirators. We could barely contain ourselves from laughing out loud. One by one we approached the desk with our cards and presented them to Mrs. Jenkins, who glanced at them but never opened them. We were giddy with excitement afterwards.

And that was that. I'd forgotten all about it -- until now. We'd just learned from Mrs. Jenkins that Jim's mom had brought back the offensive cards and was very upset. Jim was upset too, she said. It was a very cruel thing to do, she told us as she looked around the room. He was ill and at home and now suffering from the insults. Mrs.

Jenkins was livid. She wasn't the smiling woman I knew anymore. Mine was the first hurtful birthday card out of the pack.

"Who made this card?" She held it straight up above her head as she looked around the floor making eye contact with all of us kids sitting in a semicircle around her. I'd never seen her so angry.

I felt paralyzed. What should I do? Should I lie? Stay silent? I looked around for help. The clock was ticking. Would someone else give me away? I felt hot and sweaty. My heart was beating furiously. I raised my hand.

"I know who wrote it," I said, in a hesitant voice. "She's home sick today but I can take it to her."

Mrs. Jenkins' eyes opened wide as her mouth dropped open.

"*Amanda!?*" She cried, her tone full of shock and disappointment. My name seemed to just hang suspended in midair above me. Mrs. Jenkins looked crestfallen.

I continued to sit on the floor in a daze. What happened next? The images are out of focus and the words are distorted. My eyes felt blurry and my blood was pumping so quickly in my ears that I could barely hear. One by one, all of the nasty birthday cards were held up and my friends had to confess.

I know there must have been consequences as a result of our actions, but I don't remember them. Did we redo our cards and send apology cards as well? Were our parents notified? Did we do detention? While I can't recall any of that now, I still do remember what hurt me the most: the feeling of my falling from grace in Mrs. Jenkins' eyes.

Psychic Session

ere's the book," she says, sliding the heavy laminated binder across the registration desk. "Pick any one with a yellow tab. They're all free now." The receptionist is heavy, in her late 60s, with wiry gray hair and an abrupt manner.

"Okay," I say tentatively as I open the binder and look for the yellow sticky tabs marking the bios of several strangers. They look like acting headshots – smiling faces that seem to say, "pick me." The three available now are all women: one blonde, two brunette, and all under fifty.

I've never picked a psychic out of a book before. I did have my stars read once. I've also been to a few healers. But this is a new experience. It's hard to figure out what my criteria should be.

I'm in Sedona, Arizona at the Center for The New Age. It's a colorfully painted, old, two-story house with an extensive store on the ground floor full of crystals, books, and assorted spiritual bric-a-brac. Upstairs are tiny rooms used for consultations. I'm on a two-hour break during an all-day tour of the area with my husband's family. We're a group of fifteen. At lunch, I announced I would be getting a psychic reading somewhere in town during our free time and asked if anyone wanted to join me. No one did.

"Come on guys," I urged the group. "It will be fun and interesting. So many people have readings here. It's a *thing* here."

Still no takers.

On my way out, one of my sisters-in-law said in a hushed tone, "I'm afraid of what they might say." That struck me. I realized some people don't believe at all, while others believe too much. The power of suggestion can be harmful in the wrong hands, but here I was in a physic hot spot and I wasn't going to let the opportunity pass. I'm a searcher by nature.

Sedona is known for its spiritual "vortexes," areas of higher energy believed to be healing and restorative. The whole town has a granola, hippie-vibe that I really like, and it's full of new agers, hikers, yogis and meditators. It's also home to millionaires because of its staggering natural beauty.

"Whatever you do, *definitely* get a reading up there," my friend Danielle said to me when we met for coffee in Scottsdale earlier that week. She lives there and is a searcher like me, always interested in learning and experiencing new things.

"Absolutely," I promised while stirring my decaf, chai, soy latte at the latest popular breakfast spot.

Now standing at the desk with the binder before me, I was confused. Some psychics used tarot cards, others used crystals, and still others used auras. I texted Danielle.

"SOS. What kind of reading should I book? I'm here now."

"Aura, psychic." She texted me back.

"Ok," I told the receptionist. "I'll go with Veronica for a half hour session."

Turns out that customers are able to book fifteen, thirty, forty-five minute or one-hour sessions on the spot. One minute later, Veronica and I are in her room. She has brown, long hair. She's friendly, attractive and looks to be about thirty. After ushering me in to sit on her sofa, she sits barefoot and cross-legged in a very comfy chair across from me. It's a small, simple room on the second floor with a window facing some treetops. It's peaceful.

She explains that she's going to be quiet for a few minutes and "read my aura and energy." I take a deep breath and relax. I feel comfortable and eager to make the most of our brief time together.

And so we begin. Here are the highlights: Turns out, I'm an old soul who has lived many lives. Veronica says I've had my struggles in this life and other lives as well, so I must have fun – now -- in this life. She looks at me seriously, smiles and says again: "Have some fun this time around, Amanda."

I feel myself exhale deeply. What wonderful news! I've earned the right to enjoy this lifetime. Sounds like I've had some tough ones too though, which is a bit scary. I feel my brow furrow but don't have time to think about it before she gives me another gem.

"You're also a bit psychic, she says. "You have gifts. Have you noticed this?" Veronica asks.

I thought about the times I'd known something was going to happen before it did. I'd rarely mentioned this to others. What I feared had come to pass several times, just as I'd imagined it. I'd never called it psychic; I called it intuition. My "knowing" has manifested itself in being able to judge character and to sometimes predict how someone was going to harm me in the future. In the past, I'd categorized these feelings as needless worrying and tried to brush them aside.

"You have strong intuition and are also a healer," Veronica says.

"This is great news," I respond, smiling. I didn't think of myself as a healer; however, I began to look back and see how it might be true. I can be a fierce and loyal health advocate for those I love. I'm also a supportive friend and many seek my advice. I'd considered majoring in psychology in college, and perhaps had missed my calling. All of this ran through my mind.

"You must trust your instinct and intuition." She raised her eyebrows.

Then she looked at my feet for several seconds.

"Your feet are very open."

I look down. My feet always opened out; so much so, that when I was a toddler, in my crib at night I had to wear shoes with a metal bar attached between them to try to turn them inward.

"You must work on grounding your feet to the earth," Veronica went on. "There's no need for full body massages in a time pinch. For you, foot massages will be just as beneficial and faster. You need them because you must ground yourself. If you go into your head too much, you will not trust your instincts; you will talk yourself out of your intuition. You must walk barefoot whenever possible and connect with the ground."

I took another deep breath and considered her sagacity. How many times had I talked myself into what I knew was wrong for me? The answer was: too many to count. This gal was on to something! The fact that I'd never met her before and would likely never see her again made her insights even more compelling. I needed to *be still and know.*

As I write this, I'm sitting barefoot with my soles flat on the ground, ready for fun.

Matchmaker

I feel like a mail-order bride.

I'm on a blind date set up by a professional matchmaker. We're meeting for a drink at the King Cole Bar in the St. Regis Hotel in New York City.

"Amanda, truth be told, I've been trying to meet you for a year," he says. "I told Andrea I wouldn't sign on with her matchmaking firm unless she introduced me to you."

This is news to me. No wonder Andrea was so persistent with me.

"You won't pay a thing. It's only the male clients that pay me," she said to me on the phone. It's 1998. I am single and work for CNBC Business News as a television reporter and fill-in anchorwoman.

"Why would I want to do this? I ask.

"My clients are great guys. This service is very exclusive. Why not just try it? You have nothing to lose."

Eventually she wore me down. So here I am sitting across from "Bachelor Number One." Just like the dating game.

"I watch you on television," he flashes a broad smile at me. He's in his forties, unusually tall at 6'6", with a big personality. He's very animated. I'm flattered but a bit uncomfortable; the fact that he "selected" me so long ago is a bit unsettling.

"It's nice to meet you too," I say.

He's high energy. I notice he's jiggling his foot while we talk and periodically scanning the crowd. He has a bony, kind face, somewhat stooped posture from being so tall, and brown hair with lots of grey mixed in. The height is imposing, but he's warm and funny. He also seems a bit edgy and restless.

We end up going out a half a dozen times during a six-month period. It turns out, he's from a wealthy family and runs part of the family business. Everywhere we go he seems to know people. He's always shaking hands and introducing me.

On our first dinner date, we ate at the original Il Mulino restaurant in the village -- without reservations. He simply made a call while enroute, and in we went to the best table no less.

"How did you do that?" I ask, as we're ushered in by the maître d.

"I'm friends with the owner," he says.

"Lucky you." I say settling in for a great meal.

I'm impressed but also suspicious. Something about that kind of "insider" type of guy makes me uneasy. He's too slick. Maybe he has mafia ties? Or maybe it's just he's too old for me; not just in age, but also in style. He definitely runs in a different social circle. Even the constant glad-handing has an old-world vibe to it.

I decide I don't have to make sense of it right now. I relax and enjoy the meal. He loves to "over order." I really love that in a dinner date, and tell him so.

"You're funny," he says.

"Thanks," I say.

On our next date, we sit courtside at the Knicks. He insists on buying me all kinds of souvenirs despite my protests. He's the type who likes to make grand gestures.

"Thank you so much but I really don't need this," I say gesturing at all the basketball swag now dropped on my lap. He just smiles.

A few weeks later, I run into him by chance at Bemelmans Bar in the Carlyle Hotel. I'm out with a group of friends visiting from San Francisco. He's alone. He is very personable and gracious, and insists on buying everyone drinks and toasting to my health. It's hard not to like him. It's very flattering.

"That guy really likes you," my friend Christian whispered in my ear after the toast.

"I really don't know him well," I said quietly. "We've only been out a few times."

I had to admit he was making a strong impression on me though. I liked his over-the-top style and exuberant energy. I hoped we could remain friends even if it didn't become a romance.

"No matter what happens in our lives, we should always stay friends and have dinner once a year at Il Mulino," I suggest one night during yet another fabulous dinner there.

"Absolutely," he says grinning at me, and touching his glass to mine.

But even as I am enjoying these first-class outings, I feel uneasy.

One night, he drove us downtown in his large white Mercedes. It must have been custom built to accommodate his height. I was lost in the front passenger seat; my feet barely touching the floor. He was an absolutely crazy driver; recklessly speeding while talking and looking over at me on the FDR drive. I felt like Diana Ross in the 70s' movie *Mahogany*, when her suicidal paramour photographer speeds down the highway taking photos of her. She's screaming at him to watch where he's going. She's terrified but he won't stop, and they eventually crash.

My knuckles grip the handrail on the door as I brace myself for impact just like she did in the movie.

"Please slow down," I cry. "And keep your eyes on the road. You're scaring me!"

"You worry too much," he said, looking over at me yet again unperturbed. It was hopeless.

A few weeks later, we're in another car -- this time with a driver -- heading to dinner.

"Hey, do you mind if we stop for a minute on the way?" he asks.

"No, of course," I say.

The next thing I know, we pull up outside a derelict building near the FDR. The driver and I end up waiting more than 20 minutes. When he finally comes back, he sinks into his seat and says, "Let's go," with no explanation.

"Were you meeting with your bookie?" I ask straight-faced. I'm annoyed now and can't resist. He just laughs and doesn't explain.

A few weeks later, at yet another Knicks' game, he gives me some memorable advice:

"Amanda, you should dress to show off your figure," he says during halftime. The entire Knicks cheerleading team is performing a bodacious dance of cleavage three feet in front of us.

"I think I dress very well," I say defensively. I look down (no cleavage showing) and adjust my skirt. I feel like a prude compared to the cheerleaders.

"You should show your body more." He nods, scanning me with his eyes, which are now twinkling with merriment.

"Humph," I snort. My feelings are hurt. I don't like hearing that I'm not enough as I am. Honestly, though, maybe he's right? I don't try to look sexy. Not that I look dumpy by any means. I just am not dressing for a man by showing off my body in tight clothing or revealing necklines. Why don't I show my figure off more? I have a good figure. He's making me *think*.

But mostly it was what he made me *feel* that troubled me. How did he know so many people? What did he do in that old building? Why was he so hyper all the time? Something about him raised red flags within me. I felt a lack of transparency. I couldn't seem to make sense of his world. In sum, I felt I didn't understand him and, as a result, I didn't feel secure with him. That, coupled with the lack of physical attraction made me realize it would never work.

Once, just before the end of the relationship, I went to his Upper East Side triplex, which was tastefully and professionally decorated, and full of valuable sports memorabilia. He had played professional basketball overseas when he was younger. After showing me his collectibles, he made a romantic overture. I wasn't comfortable and hurried out making an excuse. Before I left, he looked me in the eye.

"You should let someone love you before it's too late, Amanda."

I was a bit shocked and embarrassed by that comment, but again he made me *think*. I smiled, thanked him and left. He was always a gentleman and I appreciated it.

And so, it was with great sadness that I learned ten years later that he reportedly died of a drug overdose after years of battling serious drug problems. Perhaps that explained his odd behavior? Did we stop for him to buy drugs that night at the derelict building? I was naïve to such things at the time, yet knew something was not right. Clearly, he had his demons. While I couldn't put my finger on it then, my intuition kept me guarded and safe. I was thankful for that, but terribly sad for him. While we weren't a "match," we did make a connection and I've never forgotten him. To this day, I still think of him fondly every time I eat at Il Mulino; that is, when I can get a reservation.

My Motto

I'd rather regret the things I've done than the things I didn't do.

I'm not sure when I first read this saying, but I do know it made a big impression on me. Yes, I thought then and still do, that's what I believe and that's how I'd like to live! I'd rather do something and regret it, than not do something and regret it, especially when it comes to jewelry.

I wish I'd heard it earlier. One thing I do *very much* regret, and probably wouldn't have if I'd adopted this motto sooner, is not buying a necklace at auction at Christie's a decade ago. It was antique, most likely 18th century, with small rose cut diamonds set in pale, faded enamel surrounds of yellow, blue and pink, stationed on two delicate draping chains. The chains met in the middle, attaching to an oval, pink enameled plaque, which had a floral design in its center. Two cushion-shaped diamonds represented flower blossoms in a basket, with tiny diamonds making up the stems and the basket itself. If you flipped the pendant over, there was another floral arrangement set in dark blue enamel. That side would never be visible to others, as the necklace was not reversible; it was a private thrill for the owner alone. The necklace was something I imaged Marie Antoinette might have worn. It was quaint by today's standards and very youthful. It was delicate, feminine and antiquated. The necklace was short and could fit only a slender neck.

After seeing it in the auction catalog, I went to the preview to try it on. It was love at first sight. I felt that tingling, dizzying feeling of falling in love with a piece of jewelry. It's an unmistakable feeling for me. I can hardly think because I'm so excited. Sometimes I feel a bit faint. I try to hide this from sellers by downplaying how much I like a piece and asking a lot of questions about it, but I know instantly when I'm hooked. In an auction context, this condition leads to obsession and fear of loss, knowing I must win it or risk losing it forever. No shopping experience is as stressful and, at the same time, as exhilarating.

Auction houses publish a price range for each piece, letting potential buyers know what they think the piece is worth. Often a piece cannot be sold for less than the low price they set (this is known as the "reserve" price). The low estimate is usually the starting point of the bidding. Auction houses purposely give low estimates in order to entice potential buyers to bid. In this case, the low estimate was *fifteen thousand dollars and the high was twenty thousand dollars.* I had never bid on such an expensive piece before.

The day of the auction, I arrived early, registered, and received my numbered paddle. I found a seat near the front of the room thinking I would have a clear view of the action. I was new to the auction world then and didn't yet know that sitting in the front is not ideal. I later learned that anyone who is serious sits or stands in the back so as to better see the competition and/or preserve anonymity; or better yet, bids by phone.

I was excited as I waited for the lot number. I'd worked out my various calculations on a slip of paper I kept on my lap: what each bid from the low to the high would actually cost once I calculated in the additional buyer's premium of twenty five percent, which is added to the hammer price (the bid that wins), as well as the tax. I hoped I wouldn't have much competition given the age, size and pastel sweetness of the piece. I wanted to buy the necklace at the low end of the estimate.

After waiting for an hour, the necklace finally came up for bidding.

"Now to a lovely necklace," began the auctioneer. He's standing at the podium in front of a large screen showing the necklace in all its glory.

"The bidding will begin at fifteen thousand dollars. Do I have fifteen thousand dollars?" He scans the room, which is half full.

I immediately raised my paddle.

"Thank you to the woman in front. Now, do I have sixteen thousand dollars?" The auctioneer asked.

Then came a bid from somewhere in the room behind me.

"Sixteen thousand dollars to the gentleman in the back." The auctioneer boomed.

The auction continued that way. I again raised my paddle but so did he. Back and forth we went until my numerical notations almost ran out. I finally couldn't stand it and looked back to see a large, overweight man, casually dressed, with grey hair, holding his paddle in the air. I looked at him and did my best to plead with my eyes for him stop bidding the price up. The bid was now above what I wanted to spend. Still, we continued. Back and forth we went. No one else was bidding. Even the phones were silent. My male competitor was relentless. I began to feel angry.

He's probably a dealer, I thought to myself. He is certainly never going to wear this necklace himself! Can't he see I am a woman and I obviously want it for myself? How rude he is! I can't believe him! These and other thoughts filled my head, as my arm continued to shoot up again and again.

Still the price rose. Now it was at seventeen thousand dollars.

My heart is racing. What should I do? There's not much time. Auctions require quick, decisive action. Seconds feel like an eternity.

The auctioneer is looking at me. Waiting.

Am I going to continue bidding? Is the necklace worth it? There will surely be another one at a different stage in my life, won't there? How can I justify this price?

If I win now, the necklace will cost nearly *twenty-two thousand dollars,* including the buyer's premium and tax.

One more time, I tell myself. Yes.

I raise my hand and the auctioneer nods in acceptance.

"I now have seventeen thousand with the woman in the front of the room. Do I have eighteen thousand Sir?"

Again, the man outbids me. He is now going to pay almost twenty-five thousand dollars total if I stop bidding.

The auctioneer looks to me. I shake my head no. I falter. I just can't justify this price.

"Going once, (he pauses), going twice, (he pauses even longer), SOLD to the man in the back."

The gavel drops

Gone. My necklace is gone.

I'd rather regret the things I've done than the things I haven't done.

I've never seen anything like that necklace again. I yearn for it still. It's the one that got away. I'm hoping somewhere in the world, some lucky woman has tired of it and decides to put it up for auction again. This time around, older, wiser and more self-aware, I won't stop until it's mine.

Chess Mom

From 2010 to 2012, my Mother's Day Weekends were spent at the National Elementary School Chess Championships for Kindergarten through 6th graders in various cities across the country. Each year, my son Grey and I would fly to the tournament, beginning when he was seven years old.

Grey began playing chess when he was in second grade. He started with an after-school class. As he progressed, we added a private lesson each week with a teacher named Evan. Grey was a determined and dedicated chess student. While he enjoyed the game, what he *really* loved was competition and trophies. Soon he began competing around New York City.

These tournaments took place Sunday mornings at various public schools and lasted many hours. What I remember most was the scarcity of chairs in the subterranean hallways relegated for waiting parents and caregivers. Getting a chair was like winning the lottery. Sometimes I gave up and sat down on the cold, linoleum floor. I'd fold my down jacket into a makeshift cushion and carefully sit on it, with my day's assortment of reading materials on my lap.

Waiting wasn't easy. First there was the stress of knowing your kid was competing. Then, the hours of sitting. Next, the inevitable pull of the bake sale that capitalized on the captive audience. Donuts, coffee, candy, Indian food, pizza, won tons, cannoli -- it was all there and more. The food selection at the tournaments reflected the ethnic diversity of New York City. And for those who like to shop, there were tables strewn with all kinds of chess paraphernalia. I'll admit I purchased more than my share of unnecessary chess wares out of boredom, including travel chess sets and strategy books, despite the fact that no one else in our family played.

Each time Grey played locally he accumulated points towards his overall rating, which determined his level of play when entering his next competition. Being goal oriented, he soon set his sights on national play. Thereafter, every year we would enter the National Elementary School Chess competition. Grey competed for three consecutive years in Atlanta, Dallas and Nashville.

At the national level, there are multiple days of competition or "rounds." The games take place in huge rooms in convention centers. A thousand pairs of competitors silently shake hands across the table before each round begins. Back and forth they move their pieces and start and stop their time clocks. The silence is deafening. The rules are strict. There is no talking. If there is a question, a player must raise his or her hand and a judge will come to the table and answer it. If a player declares checkmate, a judge must come around and confirm the win before the game is declared over. One by one, the games end and the players emerge from the cavernous rooms to be greeting by their anxious parents and supporters.

In 2010, when Grey was seven, he competed in his first national tournament in Atlanta. He was determined to win a trophy. In the end, he was close; he missed it by a single point. After the loss, he was lying prostrate on the thick red carpet of the hall outside the tournament room of the Hyatt Regency, sobbing. He was inconsolable. I recall thinking at that moment that perhaps he lacked the maturity to be competing at this level, and that we shouldn't have come. But he soon recovered, vowing he'd return the following year and win a trophy. He did.

Grey learned a lot from attending those tournaments. In addition to competing, players can sign up for other unique opportunities. For example, in 2010 Grey played against the reigning female world champion, Alexandra Kosteniuk in a "simul" game, during which she simultaneously played fifty players by walking around a large room where fifty chessboards were set up in a circle. As she walked, she stopped and played one move at each table before moving to the next table. Each player responded to her move by moving his or her chess piece the next time she returned to their table. Round and round she went – but not for long. The fun was seeing how long a player could survive. Grey came away impressed; I did too.

Unlike many other schools, Grey's school (Allen-Stevenson) didn't have a chess team. That meant that the school wasn't at the national competition officially and Grey wasn't participating in school team events. We did occasionally run into another player from his school but, for all intents and purposes, the only other person we met with was Evan, Grey's coach from home.

In Dallas one year, a family from The Dalton School invited us into their school's "team room" at the tournament. That's where players, parents and coaches gather to practice in between matches. It felt like a beehive. There must have been at least forty people in the room. Players had their travel sets out and were practicing, while parents stood around drinking coffee and eating donuts. It was a glimpse into the camaraderie of a group experience and interesting to compare with the dynamic of our independent situation.

While it might have been better for Grey's *chess game* to play with a school team at these tournaments, I believe it was better for his *personal development* not to. He was sheltered from the stress and expectations of others by virtue of playing for himself. I also made sure that in addition to all of the tournament events, games and practices, we had some fun. In each city, this generally meant a sightseeing adventure, including Coke World in Atlanta, The Sixth Floor Museum at Dealey Plaza in Dallas, and the Grand Ole Opry in Nashville. We also ate at great restaurants, like Pittypat's Porch in Atlanta, and The Southern in Nashville. Finally, no trip was complete without our watching in-room movies to unwind at night. I'm not sure other chess parents would have approved of my methods, but they worked well for Grey.

Although I wanted Grey to win, I was always more focused on him playing his best. I was then, and still am, in awe of his gumption and grit. He loved competing and handled the stress beautifully. I believe Grey always knew that win or lose, I was his biggest fan. Through those experiences, I witnessed Grey develop important life skills. I loved being his wingman and grew to know my son well as a result.

As the years went on, the trophies got bigger and taller – and so did Grey. Then came other interests and chess fell by the wayside. To this day, memories of being his chess mom and those trips we took together are precious to me. What better Mother's Day gift could there be than to feel important to, and at one with, your child?

FHH

Ford Hastings Holmén came into the world three and a half weeks early on the wintery morning of March 7, 2004. He was due around April Fool's Day, and as it turned out, the joke was on us and on my Park Avenue obstetrician. The good doctor had delivered our first son, Grey, the year before and was all set to deliver Ford, but Ford had other ideas.

We were in Southampton that weekend. Rob had driven Grey out; I'd gone to a friend's wedding shower and taken the Hampton Jitney. The ride was a bit bumpy.

Later that night I woke up to a pang of early labor.

"Rob, I think I'm having a contraction," I poked him in bed to wake him up.

"What? It's probably just gas." Rob said reassuringly.

"I don't know. It feels like more than gas," I said.

"But your water hasn't broken. Just try to relax," he said yawning.

An hour later, I woke him again. Between contractions, I lifted Grey from his crib and bundled him up for the five-minute drive to Southampton General. When we arrived, it was obvious I wasn't leaving.

From the moment he was born, Ford seemed to know things. He had a keen, innate intelligence. He would look up at me and knit his tiny brows as if to say, "Do you know what you're doing?" Sadly, I felt like most of the time I didn't.

"I don't really have it all together little guy. But let's keep it our secret," I said kissing his tiny cheek. He looked at me then with a resigned expression that I took to mean he'd keep my confidence against his better judgment.

When we first introduced the boys at the hospital, Ford was cooing in my arms wrapped like a little burrito. Grey's head and ears perked up like a spaniel's when he heard the unfamiliar sounds emanating from the bundle. Grey looked down at his brother with rapt interest.

It wasn't long before Ford started attracting female admirers with his je ne sais quoi. First came the series of caregivers who fell head over heels for his lush blond hair, big blue eyes, and sweet disposition. Then came the schoolgirls of St. Ignatius Loyola day nursery. From the age of three, Ford was greeted each morning by a swarm of screaming female classmates who fought to hug and kiss him. His savoir fare and "could care less" attitude only made them want him more. The extent of their passion grew to a point where the teacher had to stop it. A few days later, a very precocious girl in his class approached me at pick up. She told me how much she missed hugging Ford and how hard it was to stop. Looking over at him wistfully, she added:

"You see Mrs. Holmén, it's just that he's so attractive."

"I understand completely," I told her. And I did.

Sometimes Ford would be distracted while watching television and absentmindedly trace his finger on the top my hand. It felt to me as if a rare and beautiful butterfly had landed on me. I barely breathed.

When Ford was five, he and I were walking on 79th street. A very patrician, older woman wearing a fur coat and hat was walking towards us. She stopped and gave Ford a head-to-toe look. Then she turned to me and said in a neutral tone:

"He's a good one. You can always tell."

It was the kind of honest assessment you'd give after inspecting a melon. She was absolutely right. He's a good one.

Memories of Paris

*I*n 1979, the dining room of the Hotel Ritz in Paris was a classically elegant jewel box in tones of buttercream and gold. The room was surrounded with antique-mirrored alcoves hung with floral paintings. Swags and jabots of opulent fabric framed the windows. Crystal chandeliers and wall sconces reflected light seemingly forever, due to a "hall of mirrors" effect. A beautiful, hand-painted mural of pale blue sky and clouds graced the oval ceiling, surrounded by carved scrolls in gilded wood. Tufted banquettes in pale pink fabric, sumptuously padded chairs, and fragrant flower arrangements completed the stately decor.

Adding to the rarified atmosphere were the half-dozen white-gloved waiters, in turn silently standing at attention or moving around the dining room, their footsteps muffled by the thick carpet.

Along the side of the room without windows, in the far-right corner, was the entrance to the kitchen where the waiters came in and out through a swinging door. This portal was hidden from view by a large decorative screen – that is, unless you were in a position to look into the far back mirror and see the reflection of what was going on behind the screen. We happened to be in that position. The dining room was almost empty; just the three of us facing inward towards the back wall of mirrors, and another party of two seated nearby, facing the opposite way.

It was my first trip to Paris. I was fifteen. I was traveling with my mother and sister, Allison, who was seventeen. It was a summer trip, a "grand tour" that included France, England and Italy. That evening as I sat admiring the beauty of the dining room, I was also a little bored. A trio of three young waiters changed that.

When they interacted with us, they were very formal. But when they slipped behind the screen, it was another story. In a nanosecond, they began playing around. Their posture, manner and silent banter reminded me of children misbehaving. From my seat, I happened to have a perfect view of their comical antics. They pretended to drop trays, run a race, and wrestle. One waiter even threw a bread roll at another's head and it bounced off. When they thought they were hidden, they were naughty boys; however, the moment they reappeared from behind the screen, they once again became the liveried servants of the Ritz dining room. Their facial expressions changed from smiling and gaping, to serious and serene.

Finally, an entertaining dinner! I decided to share the news.

"Look behind the screen at the waiters," I whispered to my mom and sister across the table.

"I can't believe this," Allison said, watching them. "It's hilarious."

"Certainly not what you would expect at the Ritz," my mom said, less enthusiastically.

That was true. But she wasn't about to stop it because we were all enjoying it. It was unexpected entertainment in an unlikely place; like watching a comedy between courses.

Life "behind the screen" was also the theme of another wonderful memory of that first trip to Paris, when I attended a Dior couture fashion show at the historic flagship store on Avenue Montaigne. The shop was housed in a stately, white mansion on beautiful tree-lined street. I remember my mother excitedly checking us in at the desk before we were ushered into a charming and intimate oval-shaped room with perhaps thirty dainty, ladylike white chairs arranged around a short runway. On each seat was a multi-paged program that contained the details and number of every outfit, as well as a pencil with which to mark off the clothes you would like to see afterwards. I was riveted. One by one, the models appeared from behind a screen, and walked the short distance down the runway, stopping, turning and pausing before slowly walking back again. The models were lithe and tall; the clients, older and well heeled. I was amazed at the number of checkmarks some of the ladies were making on their sheets. The clothes were beautiful; hand made to perfection. Some were practical; others, confections for fairy tale occasions. The show lasted about 20 minutes. For fun, I marked in my pamphlet the clothes I wished I could buy.

Afterwards, the three of us went into another room behind the screen, to see the models wearing the clothes my mother had marked of interest. The models silently turned this way and that for her, showing off the angles and intricacies of each piece as the head saleswomen instructed them in French. There was no trying on. If you wanted the outfit, you would be fitted for it and it would be made to order for you. I recall thinking how wonderful it would be to shop this way! The prices were astronomical though; I'm not sure my mother even bought any. She wasn't a socialite; but rather, spent most of her time in suits, working as an attorney in and out of court. And while she did shop frequently and bought designer clothes, she wasn't an haute-couture client. I believe we were just there for the experience, and I was grateful to her for taking us. It was the ultimate introduction to the rarified world of high fashion.

I'd always loved clothes and the show elevated my interest. From then on, I faithfully read fashion magazines including Vogue and Harper's Bazaar. While I've attended fashion shows since, they've all paled in comparison. It was the exclusivity of that day at Dior that I adored. It was yet another view "behind the screen," and an indelible memory of Paris.

Chuck E. Cheese's

"M om, *please, please* can we go to Chuck E. Cheese's?"

I glance into my rearview mirror at my adorable, towheaded sons, ages four and five, in the back seat. It's late afternoon on a Sunday in June and we're heading back into the city after a weekend in the Hamptons.

"Sure we can boys!" I say smiling to myself. It was so easy to make them happy. "Of course, let's go!"

"Yay, hurray!" the boys exclaim, clapping their hands in excitement.

I'm still smiling as I veer off the freeway, taking the exit ramp toward our destination: a pizza parlor and amusement arcade for kids. I never say no when it comes to taking them there and I have my reasons.

In all began in 2002. I was working as a television reporter for Court Television Network. The job had me covering high-profile cases across the country. We'd broadcast the courtroom action live and report on it throughout the day.

That September, I was assigned to cover a month-long criminal case in Bradenton, Florida. It was a first-degree murder and arson case. The defendants, Derek and Alex King, were brothers. They were accused of murdering their father as he slept in his recliner in the living room of their ramshackle Pensacola home. It was alleged they bludgeoned him from the back with a baseball bat before setting the house on fire. If convicted, they faced 22 years to life on the murder charge, and 30 years on the arson charge. Adding to the sensational nature of the case was the fact that the boys were just 12 and 13 years old at the time.

Murder was the lifeblood of Court TV, and by that time I'd covered a lot of it. But this time, watching the defendants in court I couldn't help thinking about my own life. I was five months pregnant with my first child. I took an extra interest in what could have made these two young brothers commit such a heinous crime.

Many witnesses took the stand, but the testimony of the boys was critical. According to the testimony, one of the brothers allegedly planned the murder, the other wielded the bat. Both set the house on fire.

What would make the boys do such a thing? It turned out that, among other things, the boys were furious because their father refused to take them to Chuck E. Cheese's that night.

After that fact came to light, the court took a 15-minute recess. I was heading out the door to get some fresh air, when my cellphone rang.

"Amanda, it's Mary from Dr. Moss' office. We have your amino results."

"Oh my gosh. Let me just sit down." I'd been waiting on pins and needles for these test results for weeks. I found the nearest bench outside the courthouse and gathered myself. My heart felt like it was racing.

"Okay, I'm ready. Is everything okay?"

"Everything is normal, perfectly normal," she said.

"Thank God," I said. I felt relief sweep over me.

"Would you like to know the sex?" she asked. "We know it now."

"Yes, yes I would," I said taking a deep breath. My husband Rob and I had already decided we'd find out ahead of time.

"It's a boy!" She said.

Wow, a boy! A boy. A son. I took a few seconds to absorb it.

I thanked her and hung up, then sat for a few moments longer looking at the palm trees, processing it all. I was elated, but the irony of the courtroom drama wasn't lost on me. When I surfaced from my reverie, I called Rob in New York to share the news.

"Are you happy?" Rob asked, sensing my hesitation. Just then my producer flagged me that it was time to head back into the courtroom. I stood up and started quickly walking back to the courthouse while still talking to Rob.

"I am, I am, of course, I'm thrilled… it's just, I'm telling you right now, our kid is going Chuck E. Cheese's whenever he wants!

Postscript: The King brothers were convicted on both counts. The verdicts were later overturned due to procedural irregularities. They then pled guilty to reduced charges of 2nd degree murder and arson. Derek and Alex King served eight and seven years in state prison, respectively.

Claustrophobia

*B*athrooms, elevators, subways, and airplanes –- at times, these are the banes of my existence because I suffer from claustrophobia.

It began more than two decades ago. I was locked in a bathroom stall without a crawl space below the door, or any open space above. It's always the same: First, I start to panic. I feel my heart racing. Next, I try again to unlock the door with shaking hands. Then I try frantically to open the door. With every attempt that fails, I become short of breath and my temperature rises. If a minute or so passes, I need to loosen my clothing. Sometimes it's so bad that I strip down to my bra. This extreme panic only happens when I'm in a bathroom that's like a closet; it's better in a stall with open high and low crawl spaces.

Once, about nine years ago in Italy, my husband had arranged for a family boat ride. I decided to take my sons, ages five and six, into the ladies' room with me before we left to meet my husband at the dock. My boys were waiting inside the ladies' lounge, and I went inside the bathroom stall. Each stall was wood paneled and private with marble floors and no space above or below the door. I must have locked the door because I was preoccupied with getting to the dock quickly. When I tried to open it, I couldn't. Panic washed over me. I called to the boys from inside what felt like a cell at that moment, to get help from the front desk. Knowing they were outside, and I couldn't watch them heightened my anxiety. Plus, they didn't speak Italian. They understood what they needed to do though, and a few minutes later two Italian men from the front desk came in and tried to assist me. We were able to communicate and they tried to walk me through unlocking the door. I was so flustered that a handyman was called in to assist. Twenty minutes later, my husband (who realized something was wrong and returned to the hotel), the boys, the head of the desk, and the handyman all greeted me when I emerged from the stall, shaking and drained.

When I close and lock any bathroom door now, after testing it a few times, all I can think about is whether or not I will be able to open it again. Because of that, I usually don't lock them and spend the whole time in a "Twister-game" type position, trying to block the door from opening with one foot and/or hand, while at the same time trying to take care of business. Sometimes the toilet is just too far away from the door. Usually, I risk it and forego the lock. I feel a lot better -- until someone walks in. Then, I apologize sincerely to the embarrassed person and explain my situation.

The problem isn't just limited to bathrooms though. Elevators are a fact of New York City life. I went to see a therapist about this issue, and she said that I must face my fears. She told me that I must continue to take them regardless of my feelings. I do take elevators generally, but draw the line at small ones in town houses, old buildings and European hotels. If I can walk instead, I always do. I'm also not a fan of going to the top of skyscrapers. A few years ago, a cousin had his wedding reception at the top of the highest building in Dallas. The thought of being stuck in that elevator filled me with dread. I dug deep to find my courage, and made it to the top.

But it's not just being stuck above ground that rattles me. The subway is also a challenge. I'm okay while it's moving, but the moment the conductor says we are being held indefinitely for a mechanical problem or because of train traffic, my anxiety kicks in. The last time it happened, on my way to the Tenement Museum in lower Manhattan, I felt the need to talk to the young woman seated next me to try and stem my rising panic. She, however, lacked a comforting bedside manner.

"You really have to get over that," she said looking grumpy and bored.

"I know," was all I could come up with to say.

I should always carry water and Valium with me. Usually, I do whenever I fly. Flying itself is no problem; it's being trapped on a stopped plane that triggers my reaction. The worst experience I've ever had was when I was flying with my two young sons to San Francisco about ten years ago. The flight was delayed for about four hours in the airport. Then after boarding, we proceeded to sit there for another four without moving from the gate. During that time, I took Valium but felt increasingly panicked. When the plane finally moved, it pulled back a few feet from the terminal only to stop again. We continued to wait. Finally, hours later, sweating and shaking, I told the flight attendant that I needed to deplane.

"But we *really* are just about to leave," she told me.

"I just can't make a six-hour flight after five hours of waiting. I'm having a panic attack."

"You're going to have to speak with the pilot at this point, Miss."

"Okay," I said.

The pilot was a lot nicer and agreed to return to the gate. After making a quick announcement, the plane returned to the gate and the door was opened.

I woke the boys, who were sleeping peacefully.

"Are we in California?" my older son Grey asked. Their eyes were still hazy from sleep.

"No guys. Sorry, we are still in New York. We'll try again tomorrow."

The three of us began our slow walk of shame up the aisle toward the front of the plane. As I passed by, dozens of angry passengers glared at me.

"You better be *really* sick," a surly lady hissed at me.

"Yeah, hard to believe your whole family is sick, even your husband," someone else jumped in.

I looked back to see a tall man trailing behind me. His eyes were rimmed in red, and he was covered in sweat. I gave him a sympathetic smile. He looked worse than I did. We all walked off the plane together - one big, happy, neurotic family.

The first thing I did was go back to the United Airline's desk and see if I could get a seat on the first plane out the next day.

"You're first in line," the counter gal said.

"Well, I just got off Flight 762 to San Francisco and need to rebook."

"That entire flight's been cancelled," she said.

"What?" That was news to me. It turned out they'd exceeded their flight crew's maximum non-flying shift time.

When I called my husband from the taxi heading home, he was incredulous and angry.

"You can't just turn a plane back! You could be arrested or something!" Rob said.

"No, you can't be arrested if you're feeling sick! This is the first time in my life I've ever had to do anything like this! I had a serious panic attack. I just couldn't do it. And I wasn't the only passenger who felt that way," I replied defensively.

The next day, we again boarded the plane with many of the same people who were hostile to me the night before.

"I hope you're feeling better," a woman said rolling her eyes.

"Yes, thank you. In fact, I am." I held my head high and tried to ignore the sarcasm in her voice. Let's just say the airline's advertising did not live up to its name that day: I did not experience the "friendly skies of United."

❧

Lonely Bench

The lonely, yet lovely, bench sat unused, gracing the foyer with its presence. Its gilt gold hue and caned seat were well worn with more than a century of age. It was shaped like a crescent, with arms and legs curved and accented with scrolls and swags. A sweet antique from a long, lost era; impractical as it was charming.

Nineteen years ago, as I walked through the myriad of antique shops in Porte de Clignancourt outside of Paris, the Belle époque bench caught my eye. Not one to concern myself with the practical, I immediately fell in love and bought it. Soon after, it arrived in New York City along with some other fine purchases I made, following a sea voyage and clearing customs.

Soon the little beauty had pride of place in my apartment. Single and carefree at the time, I placed it in my foyer underneath a stately mirror and enjoyed seeing it each and every day. It cheered me to no end. I'd set my handbag or scarf on it when I came in after work. No heavy lifting for this bench.

When I married and had children, I continued to mother the little belle bench. It still sat in a place of pride in the foyer, beneath my beautiful mirror. It was understood by everyone that it was not to be used as a bench – ever. I told the boys when they were little that although it looked like a bench, and was where a bench should be, it was never to be used as one. They were innocent and trusting and nodded solemnly.

As the boys grew up, the little bench stayed put. I'd explain to their friends on play dates that it wasn't to be sat on. As the children got older, they would explain that to their friends themselves. I appreciated their cooperation and compliance. I don't recall them asking me why, but they knew it was from France and very old. I imagine they also just decided it must be a "girl thing."

Without realizing it, I later made my little jewel even more tempting by having a custom toile cushion with piping made to fit it. It looked so elegant! My husband and two sons just shrugged when they saw it. Again, no questions. Once in a while, though, my husband would ask me if we might want to replace it with a real, functioning bench. Usually, he would ask while balancing on one leg trying to pull off a rain boot. I'd look at him with compassion and understanding before saying no; sadly, there really wasn't any better place for my gem.

Then came the fateful day, three years ago, when I'd invited a group of women for lunch. I greeted my guests at the door, and took their coats. I'd led them into the living room for drinks, and then I quickly went into the kitchen to check on lunch. When I returned, the unthinkable had happened: a heavy friend was sitting on the bench adjusting her shoe! I stood frozen; any moment the original caning would break, and my friend would fall to the floor.

Composing myself, I said lightly, "I'm so sorry. That bench shouldn't be there. It's in need of repair. Please let me assist you to get up."

I helped her up and that was that. She, and the bench, survived. But after that, I had to face the fact that my bench's "prime time" placement was up.

I found a handsome upholstered alternative that was long, wide and comfortable. It didn't look elegant but everyone, including me, was relieved. We could actually sit on it and take our shoes on and off! Imagine! We could throw backpacks, handbags, jackets and magazines on top! Even the dog joined the fun. He decided to sleep on it during the day to keep an eye of the comings and goings. To this day, no one worries about it.

The gilt bench is now in my bedroom in Southampton. It sits in a lovely place, against a wall underneath a painting. These days it's only used by me, and very gingerly; the occasional nightgown or sweater dropped upon it. I'll never forget how it bravely stood up to the test that day in New York City, but I'm glad to say those days of worrying are over. It's mine - all mine - now once again, and will stay that way: lovely but perhaps lonely.

❧

A Night to Remember

My heavy silk, teal-colored gown has intricate billowing three-quarter length sleeves, a boat neck, fitted waist and gentle mermaid shaped long skirt, with an ornate pleated ruffle that ends in a two-foot train. My hair is artfully arranged in an upward sweep; a loose bun pinned high on my head. I'm wearing my favorite diamond bracelet and ring. My long earrings match the gown. I'm wearing matching teal pumps. A sparkling gold evening bag completes my outfit. I feel like a princess who is going to the ball! I am a bit like Cinderella tonight in my rented carriage, traveling alone. My husband couldn't make it, but I wouldn't have missed it for the world. I have a long, black car waiting for me. The driver has my special pass displayed in his front windshield. Without it, we won't be allowed inside the gates. As we make our way towards our destination, I let the majesty of London sweep over me.

When we arrive, we join a line of other cars waiting to enter the grand gates. A throng of tourists stands and stares at us. They peek inside my car window and I smile back. I feel like a movie star. Before we enter the gates, I pass my invitation and the required photo identification to the driver who shows both to the guards. They nod and let us pass. Once inside the courtyard, we stop at the doorway. A footman opens the car door. My shoe touches the red carpet. I rise from the car and begin a slow and steady assent to the door and through it. I'm now inside

Buckingham Palace. After checking my phone at the makeshift cloakroom (no cellphones allowed), I begin my walk up the first long marble staircase. Everywhere I look I see white marble, gold sconces, and red carpeting. Footmen are posted along the way. When I reach the landing, I am greeted by a painting of Charles I on horseback. I tell myself to slow down, enjoy it and stay in the moment. I breathe deeply and proceed slowly. I look right to see a sweeping view of the Queen Victoria Memorial from the balcony where royals have waved and kissed following weddings. From there, I enter into a large reception hall with reddish brown marble columns and deep bluish silk wall covering. The view from this room is of the great lawn, where the queen most recently hosted a royal garden party for the man of the hour's upcoming 70th birthday.

The cocktail reception is already underway. The room is full of supporters of the Royal Philharmonia Orchestra. Prince Charles has been its Royal Patron for 40 years. We've been invited in celebration of that milestone. In total, 140 of us are here.

I'm offered canapés on silver trays and glasses of champagne. One side the room has large windows facing the lawn; the other has tapestries interspaced between ornate wall panels. Both sides are lit by multi-armed gold candelabras. The room is full of beautifully dressed women in long dresses, and men in black tie, and it's buzzing with excitement as we await the arrival of our host.

After a few minutes, Prince Charles, Duke of Wales, arrives. He carries a highball glass, filled with a clear drink and a slice of lime in his left hand, as he begins the royal "meet and greet." I'm fixated on Prince Charles as he moves systematically through the line. We stay put; he comes to us. I'm getting a bit nervous. I can't believe this is actually happening! And then it does. Suddenly, the Prince of Wales is greeting me and extending his hand. It's surreal. I'm looking into his eyes, which are a startling shade of blue; a turquoise blue, unexpectedly arresting in his ruddy face. He's cordial and formal. I congratulate him and wish him an early happy birthday. Then he's on to the next guest.

I feel myself exhale. I turn to the others in his wake, similarly, dazed by the experience. After everyone has met the Prince, we are asked to proceed to the concert hall where the orchestra will perform for us. The room is magnificent: white walls with gold and white panels, an ornate ceiling, marble carvings, and tapestries. The focal point is a red canopy in the center of the room behind the orchestra displaying a royal crest of two lions in gold. It's gathered into a corona at its apex. At the top is an arch of gold cherubs, surrounding a golden wall clock mounted in marble. Four magnificent crystal chandeliers hang from the ceiling.

When everyone is seated, the Prince arrives and takes his seat in the front row. The music and acoustics are extraordinary. The program includes music from Mozart's 'Don Giovanni' overture, Strauss' 'Don Juan', and Stravinsky's 'The Firebird.' A soprano sings. I feel rapture; I'm transported by the spectacle and surroundings. When it's over His Royal Highness speaks to us: about his patronage, his love of music, his childhood trumpet lessons and later cello playing, his great grandfather's and great, great, grandfather's bringing musicians into the court to play in this room. He speaks of how important listening to live music is. He thanks us for our support. We are asked to proceed to dinner. The Prince stays behind.

I take the opportunity to visit the ladies room, out of curiosity. The entrance is through a door in the wall disguised by wallpaper to match the walls. It's just an ordinary ladies room with four stalls, plain hand towels (no royal stamp or markings), liquid soap and lotion. The toilets flush by pressing a button on the wall. I don't dare use one; I can't risk damaging my gown.

Dinner is in the portrait gallery, an enormous room with walls lined in rose damask. We have some time before the Prince arrives, so I stroll along admiring the room's collection of masterpiece paintings, hung three in a row down from the arched ceiling above. I pass multiple Rembrandts, Van dykes, and Titians, among others. When Prince Charles arrives, we all sit. Each round table is set with silver, china, flower arrangements and large electrical candelabras with decorative beige shades with the royal insignia on them. The china is white with a gold border. The glasses are banded with gold at the top. A printed menu is displayed in the center of the table. I'm at a table with other Americans. The Prince is seated at another table in my field of vision, twenty feet away. A waiter offers me bread from a breadbasket, and when I choose one, he gestures that I should take it with my hands (quite a surprise!). We eat salmon tartare, lamb chops, and a lemon pavé and elderflower sorbet for dessert. There are four glasses: for water, champagne, wine and port. Chocolate truffles are served with coffee and tea.

Then, His Royal Highness stands, and we follow suit. He shakes hands with the dinner companions on his left and right, and then begins to walk out of the room. Before he leaves us, he says over his shoulder, "Good night, all" and waves his hand above his head, all the while looking straight ahead and continuing to walk toward the doorway and into another hallway.

Then it's time to go. I linger as I make my way down the many flights of stairs. I admire the furniture along the way (including long upholstered tufted sofas that can seat at least twenty, tables with sculptures and objéts, decorative niches with marble statues, and royal china sets displayed in glass cabinets). As I walk out of the palace doors held by liveried footmen, I stop and take in the sight of the courtyard at night and the view of the monument beyond its magnificent gates.

It's a night to remember, and remember it I will.

The Birthday Parade

I'm pretending to be asleep but I'm really wide awake. I've been up for some time now, alert with excitement. I'm waiting for signs that it's about to begin. I hear some rustling outside my room, a toilet flushing, some whispers. I shut my eyes tighter and turn on my side. I look over at the digital clock. It's 6 a.m. I've been tossing and turning for at least an hour. Waiting is hard.

The whispers are getting more frequent now. I hear heavy footsteps and paper bags crinkling. Next, I hear a slightly raised voice say, "Okay: one, two, three...." Then the door bursts open, the overhead lights snap on, and I hear the familiar chorus:

"Happy birthday to you, happy birthday to you, happy birthday dear Amanda, happy birthday to you!"

As I pretend to wake up, I open my eyes and squint and blink, adjusting to the light. I see my dad, my mom, my sister and my brother walking in, singing and bearing gifts. It's my twelfth birthday.

It's a short walk from outside the door to my bed, so the birthday singing extends longer than the walking does; it carries over while each family member plunks himself or herself down on my bed, putting the gifts in an unsteady pyramid on my lap. Some slip off onto the mattress while others fall to the floor.

Now it's my time to act surprised.

"Thanks everyone! Thanks so much. You got me this time!"

"Were you really surprised?" asks my fourteen-year-old sister, Allison.

My eleven-year-old brother, Philip, yawns. He still looks half asleep.

"Yes," I fib, not wanting to ruin the moment. The truth is no one is ever *really* asleep knowing the birthday parade is imminent.

The bed is crowded not only with my human family and gifts, but with my animals as well. Over the years, our dogs and cats have been recruited to join in the festivities. We just carry them in with us and plop them down on the bed too. They have a way of making themselves the center of it all - toppling the gifts off the bed in their fervor to claim the catbird seat. Today, that's right in the middle of my lap. This birthday, our two cats, Fenix and Felix, have joined the celebration.

I sit up against the headboard. Decisions, decisions. Which gift do I open first? What fun! I proceed to unwrap my presents. Sometimes I tear the paper; sometimes I'm like a surgeon trying to extract the gift without damaging a pretty ribbon or wrapping. I open them one by one, taking my time with everyone watching. I can tell my brother, Philip, is antsy for me to get it over with. Mom starts a garbage bag for the all the loose paper and ribbons strewn around the room. I have a few minutes to play with my gifts: a music player, a necklace, clothes, and other twelve-year-old girl delights. Then it's time to get ready for school. Another year, another parade. Next year, I'll be older, but the birthday parade never changes.

The ritual is one of my fondest memories of childhood. In fact, it *predates* my earliest memories. In our family, it was one of the few constants. Now, so many years later, I've still never met another person whose family shared this ritual.

The parade originated in my mom's family. We don't know which relative gets the credit; however, we do know that from the very start, the key was the surprise factor: it began early – at least an hour before regular alarms went off, at a time when you were ostensibly sleeping.

Years later when I lived alone, I would get a singing birthday call from my mom. It was also nice, albeit never the same as the unparalleled parade. For one thing, it wasn't a wake-up call.

And so, it was with great relish and joy that I assumed the mantle and carried on the tradition with my own sons. From their first birthdays to this day, they have woken up to the birthday parade. I have also taken it a bit further. When I was growing up, we didn't have birthday parades for our parents; now, in our family we do. I wanted the boys to feel the excitement of getting woken up early to prepare in the dark for the under-cover missions.

This year, for the first time, both of my boys will be away at boarding school on their birthdays. Sadly, it's the end of an era. Fortunately for Rob and me, though, our birthdays fall in mid to late December when the boys will be home from school, so the tradition will carry on. For the boys' birthdays, it's now time to employ the second-best option: the singing birthday phone call. Again, I plan to tweak tradition: I don't want to just call singing, I want to *wake them up* singing, just like the good old days of their youth! I just need to figure out how early to call. They won't be expecting it; they've never asked what comes next after the birthday parade years.

Now *you* know, though. Let's keep it our secret.

Breast Friend

I f you want to have your boobs done, I have a great doctor in Las Vegas who does all of my dancer friends. I'll treat you too."

"Ah, no thanks. I like my breasts the way they are, thank you very much," I replied haughtily. Ryan was unlike anyone else I knew. I felt myself tense and pulled my coat tighter protectively as we walked out of the restaurant onto the street.

What a jerk, I thought to myself. He obviously doesn't appreciate my body type. I found his offer offensive, a put down, rather than a generous gesture from a misguided friend.

This was typical of Ryan. I met him in my teens on a bench in downtown San Francisco. I was on my lunch break working as a receptionist at my mom's law firm. He was working for his father's venture capital firm. We dated a bit and met each other's parents.

Ryan liked me and tried to woo me; I liked him too but didn't feel secure with him. He was often unpredictable and childish, and I wasn't sure I could trust him as a boyfriend. He paid me the highest compliment one day when he called me a "watermelon seed."

"Whenever I try to get close, you slip away," he said, gesturing the pinching motion with his fingers. I just laughed, delighted. He was good for my ego and lots of fun. Most of the time.

Fast forward to my freshman year at Northwestern University. Ryan called me with an invitation. His friend, the son of the owner of a large family publishing firm, was having a lavish black-tie party in a northern suburb of Chicago. Would I accompany him? He was flying out from California for it. "Of course." I said. I remember like yesterday the grand estate, the mansion, the sumptuous table laden with sliver, the candles, the antique mirrors and, when I went the wrong way down a labyrinthine hallway trying to find the powder room, finding Reid instead in a corner with another woman canoodling and writing down her phone number. I felt like I'd found my husband cheating on me. I was livid. I was humiliated. In retrospect, I wonder why I reacted so strongly. We weren't lovers. We weren't committed. Yet, I was his date and he had embarrassed me and hurt my feelings by pursuing someone else at the party behind my back. I yelled at him and spent the rest of the night giving him the cold shoulder and trying to make him feel guilty.

In time, though, we resumed our friendship. With new ground rules established, I consented to be his date to museum galas and other events in New York City when he visited, so long as he didn't obviously scout out new dates in front of me. It worked. He wanted a date and I loved getting dressed up and going to parties. It was a win-win.

One day during lunch in New York City in our mid-thirties, we had a typically weird conversation. Ryan asked me to have his baby. His idea was that he would support the child and me completely without getting married. I could live in New York or move to California. He would stay in California. He couldn't think of anyone better to be the mother of his child, he said.

"What about love, though?" I asked. He didn't have a good answer. Again, I found his proposition irritating and sad rather than touching. I didn't want to be a kept woman raising his baby. There wasn't much in that for me. It was crazy.

My mom liked the idea though.

"He's so handsome and RICH! Why not? I'll help you with the baby."

"Mom, this is ridiculous! He doesn't LOVE me."

"So what?" she said. "It's more of a business deal."

"No, I'm not going to settle for that, but I'm glad to know you're available for cross country babysitting when the time comes," I replied sarcastically.

Instead of agreeing to have Ryan's baby, though, I did go to Las Vegas with him and two of his friends, a married couple, for the weekend.

The four of us were having a grand time at a trendy restaurant when Ryan said, "I have an announcement to make."

"Oh my God, you're getting married, aren't you?" exclaimed the wife. I didn't know what was going to come out of Ryan's mouth.

"No," he said, "Amanda and I are going to see *Madonna* in concert tonight!"

He was full of surprises and grand gestures. For many years, he'd call whenever he was in New York. Once we headed out to Montauk with a trunk full of tiki torches. Ryan was an excuse to let go, have fun and be crazy in my own way. Just agreeing to spend time with him was giving myself permission to expect the unexpected.

In our thirties, he continued to act like a fraternity boy. I told him to be careful and called him "the patron saint of Las Vegas showgirls." He'd take a gaggle of them away on vacation to Hawaii and elsewhere, let them charge up a storm at the hotel and pay for their cosmetic procedures when they got home. I was worried for him.

"You're behaving like a trust fund idiot," I told him. "You're being used." He just laughed. I think he was having too much fun to care.

Years later, a newly divorced and weepy me, and a still-single Ryan had lunch in New York City. He insisted on taking me shopping after lunch, an activity no man before or since has suggested. I said 'no' (like I believed a lady should) several times but he wore me down (which wasn't that hard, let's be honest). He said to pick my favorite store. It was Max Mara. Three coats later, I really did feel much better. It wasn't like me to accept that kind of generosity, but after so many years of friendship I figured it was okay. After all, if I didn't accept, the money would go toward some other girl's tits. That afternoon was followed by a call from my financial advisor informing me of an unexpected gift of stock from Ryan.

"To make you feel better," he said when I called stunned.

At that moment, he was my breast friend after all.

The Sweater

I stared at the sweater a long time, trying to decide whether or not to keep it for what seemed like the hundredth time. It was a thirty-year-old, black cashmere cardigan with small, shiny black beads stitched along the round collar and down the front edges. Conservative, a bit dressy, and a reminder of a lost relationship. I didn't remember ever wearing it. I put it on and looked at myself in the full-length mirror turning from front to back. Nothing special about it. Why keep things that make me feel sad? That's it. Goodbye. I placed it on the top of an overflowing bag of clothes to donate to the charity store down the street.

The next morning there it was on the top of the bag again, daring me to let go of the past. My hand reached out to touch it. It was the last thing I owned that my sister Allison had given me. So much water under the bridge. So much hurt.

My mind flashed back to a phone conversation during my divorce twenty years earlier. I felt low and destabilized. I was talking with Allison about it – about the loss of love.

"Well, at least you love me," I said off the top of my head.

The phone line went silent. More than a pause went by, then a lot more than that – more than I could bear.

Please respond, please respond! No, this isn't happening. I felt clammy, panic rising.

"Hello? Are you still there?" The silence was intolerable. I couldn't let it go on a single second longer. I was alert to every sound, and the silence was deafening.

"I'm thinking," she said.

My throat tightened and my eyes watered. How was it possible someone could be so mean? Why was this okay? It's another one of those silent stabs - the moments I know I will never forget. She doesn't love me and never will, at least not how I want her to. I feel I don't deserve this. I change the subject and get off the phone as soon as possible. I don't know what to do next. What to think? What to feel? Honesty kills.

Months later, at Christmas she gave me a Baccarat crystal heart. "An answer to your question," she said. It did nothing to repair the damage. An intellectual Band-Aid. Not nearly enough for me. Too little, too late. Not that she'd notice.

That's how it was with her and me. She was just "being honest." She wanted boundaries and privacy, while I wanted closeness and communion. This difference in our makeup belied our shared DNA, always.

Once I asked if I could feel her pregnant belly. We were shopping together at a maternity store in a mall. She was in a dressing room. She was the older sister and I'd never felt someone's pregnant stomach. Surely, she'd let me? "No," she snapped. "It's my body. You don't know what it's like to feel fat." This, from a woman who was always rail thin.

How to explain I wanted to feel close, to share something amazing? My cheeks reddened from the sting of her words, as much as if she'd hit me there.

My fingers are still touching the black fibers, debating. I pull the cardigan from the bag and hang in back up in my closet.

I'm going to lunch with a new friend today near my apartment on the Upper East Side of Manhattan. It's a lovely, warm, fall day. Still, restaurants can be chilly. On an impulse, I grab the black sweater even though it's dressy with all the beads. I put it on. I walk to the restaurant and arrive a bit early. I'm waiting by the bar. I'm facing the door and a wall of windows, which backlight the people walking in. I'm looking for my friend who is a tall, strawberry blonde.

Suddenly, I see someone else approaching the bar. She's familiar. Very familiar. It's been more than five years since I've seen her, but I recognize her instantly: my sister. The last time I saw her was in Palm Beach. I ran into her and her son in a department store and asked if we could all get together, have lunch and talk.

"My boys and I are staying in Palm Beach for the week. It would be great to get the cousins together," I said.

"Let me think about it," she said, her voice full of false friendliness.

She never called.

I walk toward her now.

"Allison," I hear myself say. "It's been a long time." As far as I know, she still splits her time between Florida and New Jersey.

"Yes," she says. "You look beautiful. You haven't changed." I'm stunned by her compliment, although it sounds more like an observation; still, I'm grateful. Her tone and demeanor are polite and reserved. We stare at each other taking in the changes that have occurred since I took "the road not taken," my "Robert Frost" moment, which separated me from my family. I'm full of questions for her, despite myself. I ask a few, but it's obvious from her succinct responses that she wants to keep it light and move on.

Suddenly I realize something. "Do you see this sweater?" I ask.

She glances at it.

"You gave it to me years ago and it's the only thing I have left from you."

"It's a *nice* sweater," she says nodding, as if confirming her good taste.

"Yes, but the reason I mention it is because I was going to give it away yesterday but for some inexplicable reason, I kept it. I haven't worn it in years because it brings up painful memories. I don't know why I wore it today. I don't know if it brought me to you, or you to me, but it's amazing!"

"That is amazing," she said smiling.

I began to ask her another question – desperate to understand more about the estrangements in our family. I don't know when I'll have the chance again.

Just then my friend walked in. I turn briefly from my sister and asked my friend to wait for just a moment. But when I turn back, my sister says she doesn't have any more time to talk. She says she feels "ambushed."

"But it's so important," I plead, flummoxed by her impending retreat.

She repeats that she has to go now to the table to meet her friend who is waiting. I acquiesce, apologizing for pushing, explaining that I just never get the chance to talk to her.

After lunch, I decide to go into the back room of the restaurant to find her. She looks startled and not pleased to see me again.

"Sorry to interrupt," I say adopting a light tone, "but we're leaving, and I wanted to say goodbye and give you a hug."

"Oh, okay," she says visibly relaxing after considering my request.

We hugged. It felt good. My sweater absorbed all of the love that was there.

I'm keeping it.

Via Venom

*I*t was an innocent mistake. Last week, I typed the wrong address into the destination on my Via app, a communal car service accessible by iPhone. It's a $5.00 ride anywhere in Manhattan; the only catch, you share the vehicle.

I got into my assigned minivan at 80th and Park around 9:30 a.m. It was just the driver and me, so I sat in the front and we chatted about the weather. He was soft-spoken, polite, perhaps Hispanic, and around forty. I casually mentioned I was getting off at 38th Street.

"Oh, I think I have you down for getting out at 19th Street," he said.

"What? Oh boy, let me check. I have a doctor's appointment."

I called information and sure enough, the doctor's office was on 38th and 1st. In the meantime, we had stopped, and two women had boarded. They weren't together – one appeared to be in her early thirties, long brown hair, a bit exotic, and dressed professionally; the other was heavy, in her sixties, casually dressed, and carrying a bag of paint cans. We turned onto the FDR. The traffic was light, and cars were moving nicely.

"Don't worry about it," I said to the driver. "My mistake."

A few minutes later, he took the next exit off the FDR.

The young woman looked up from her cellphone and started yelling, "Driver, what are you doing? You're taking the exit. We're going downtown!"

I looked back sheepishly and said, "I think he's doing something nice for me." I felt embarrassed and was hoping she'd be okay with it. She wasn't.

"What the hell are you talking about? You can't have him get off his route!"

"I didn't ask him to," I said. "I know that's not the way it works on Via."

"But you're making him do it anyway, aren't you?" She glared at me. "*Oh, I think the driver's doing something nice for me!*" She did an ugly imitation of me to my face, taunting me.

"What's going on?" the other women piped in, suddenly realizing the young woman was screaming at me.

The young one said loathingly, "She's having the driver drop her off and we're paying for it."

The younger one's voice was full of sarcasm and rage. Her dark eyes were hard, and the whites of her eyes seemed to be reddening. She was livid.

I hoped the other would disarm the tension.

"Throw her out now! Get her out of this car now," the older woman shouted. "Right now. Out! Out!"

Their words and behavior were ugly and hostile. I was having trouble processing the escalation. These seemingly normal-looking women were berating me. They were ready to tar and feather me. They literally wanted to throw me out of a moving vehicle! I felt physically and psychologically threatened. I was stunned. I saw enraged faces, fingers wagging, mouths contorted by rage. My body was absorbing the hatred on a cellular level. I was flooded with adrenaline. I needed to turn it off; it was hurting me. I turned back to face them again.

"I know this is unusual and I sincerely apologize to you both. I don't know why our driver decided to do this, but all I can say is I'm going to get out and take a cab and he can get right back on the FDR."

"You have to be the world's biggest narcissist!" shrieks the younger passenger. "I bet you get everything you want, all the time. *I can't stand yo*u." Her face looks contorted and pinched; it's getting red.

I inhale her toxic fumes. I feel dizzy. Oh my God. This is unbelievable. I square my shoulders and say serenely:

"I must really remind you of someone you hate because you don't even know me. You know nothing about me or my life." I feel my brow furrow trying to understand the personal attacks.

"I know that I hate everything about you," she says. "I even hate your voice."

I'm stunned. She's a she-devil incarnate. I try again. Ladylike. Polite.

"Wow," I say. "That's something. You were in the car the whole time, and you know I didn't ask him to do this for me. All I can say is I'm sorry for inconveniencing you."

"No, you're not," she shrieks. She's seething with venom. I try another tack.

"Can't you just chalk it up to he's doing something nice and you are too by extension and someday, someone will do something nice for you? I made a mistake. We're already off the FDR. There's nothing I can do. He's going to get back on."

"You make me sick," she practically spits at me.

I'm questioning the universe now. Never before have I felt like I was the selected one in 'Our Town,' whose turn it is to be stoned to death by townspeople. I open my wallet within my purse, considering whether to give each of them cash for their rides in an effort to get them to stop yelling at me. I'm reeling from the barrage of personal attacks and name-calling.

"I'm calling Via right now," said the older one. "You're going to pay for our rides," she said pointing her finger at me. "I paid extra for express. You'll pay for this."

"You're making us late and you don't even care!" the young one barks.

"Why is she still in the car?" the older one asks. "Driver, she needs to get out now. Just drop her anywhere! Anywhere!"

"Nobody is going to pay for the ride," the driver said calmly. It was the first time he'd spoken. "I'm going to explain this to the company. You won't be charged."

"Are you taking her to 38th street?" the older one asks. "You can' t be serious. Get back on the FDR now!"

"I'm getting back on the FDR at the next entrance point but I'm heading south on Lexington and she's getting out at 38th street – not before."

I looked over at this man. I gave him a grateful nod.

As he pulls to the curb to let me out, the younger one sticks it to me again.

"You haven't even apologized to us," she hisses. "Do it now."

"I already did but I will again." I say like the demoralized victim I am. "I'm sorry."

I thank the driver and walk away – shaken and humiliated.

A week later, I'm still reliving the trauma of the bullying. My only act: one of gratitude, having left the driver a $10 tip online for the $5 ride.

The King and I

The "King" of the television network I worked for from 2001 to 2006 was the network's president, Hank Shine. Hank was a larger-than-life character, at times charming, a real schmoozer, and a shameless self-promoter. That is to say, he was a typical, successful television network head. I was officially single when I began working at the network, but very shortly afterwards married my then boyfriend and now husband, Rob. A year later, I had my first child. Hank was always courteous to me, but what really put me on the map with him was when a friend of his mentioned that I was, "the one that got away." This friend was a major New York business fixture and philanthropist, with whom I'd had the sum total of one dinner date. So the comment, while flattering, was a joke. Still, on the rare occasion when I went to see Hank in his palatial office, he never failed to mention this. By the time I was pregnant with my second son, it was really getting old.

"You're the one that got away, Amanda. That's what Josh always says!" He'd say, flashing his very bleached, white, toothy grin.

"That's funny Hank, seeing as we had one date. But really, the reason I'm here is to talk about the anchor spot opening up."

"Yeah, yeah, yeah. Thanks for coming by; I'll think about it, really. Keep up the good work. Great job, Amanda. Just super."

I tried not to let the door hit me on my way out. By this time, I had worked at the network for years on virtually every show. While I was technically an on-air reporter, I'd filled in regularly on all of the shows as a substitute anchor. I was tired of always being the bridesmaid and never the bride. I wanted to anchor my own show.

So you can imagine my chagrin, when out of the blue another woman claimed the prized seat. Kelly was a former prosecutor from San Francisco with limited on-air experience. She'd moved across the country to take the job. The network provided voice coaches, private anchor training, taped practice sessions at night on set with full crews – everything and anything to get her up to speed.

I took it hard. I was so jealous and frustrated by what was happening at work, I used to joke to my husband that our baby would be born green. Adding insult to injury was the fact that Kelly and I had similarities: we were both from San Francisco, had both gone to law school and practiced law there, were both brunettes, and around the same age. Several times during those years, people asked me if I'd worked as a lingerie model during law school. No, I'd say, perplexed. I later learned *that* girl was none other than Kelly. For years, we worked amicably as colleagues but through no fault of her own, I could never truly befriend her. It was professional rather than personal; she'd eclipsed me, and it stung.

Her meteoric rise to the anchor desk was fueled by her biggest admirer, Hank. I'll never forget being asked to attend the opening of a film festival featuring a case we'd covered. As I walked the red carpet, several photographers took my photo before asking Hank to pose with me.

"Just a minute," he told the group. "Where's Kelly?" Only after he'd found and included her did he agree to be photographed with me.

As time went on, I looked for new opportunities to advance. The network had lost the host of its evening entertainment show and I'd filled in several times. I wanted the job. The show's producer was a big supporter of mine and voiced that. Still, no announcement came. I went to see Hank.

"Amanda, take a seat. Hey, I saw Josh the other night. You're the one that got away Amanda." I felt the need to enlighten him once again.

"It was one date Hank. He wanted me to take a cab even though his car and driver were parked at the curb waiting for him after dinner. That hardly sounds like love at first sight, does it?" He wasn't listening. I transitioned to business. I wanted the anchor spot in addition to my other duties.

"I see where you're coming from Amanda. But the truth is, you're not edgy looking enough. I'm looking for edgy. Maybe wear trendy glasses on air?"

"Okay Hank. I will next week." How interesting, I thought to myself, that Kelly had recently begun to wear fun glasses on air.

After that, I wore edgier cloths and yes, even trendy glasses when I filled in as the anchor on the show.

A month later, sitting in Hank's office, he sat back and assessed me again. Using his hands and gesturing to me as I sat there, he raised his brows.

"Amanda, you need to think 'Connecticut.' I'm looking for pink cashmere sweaters and pearls. A classy look."

Whoa. "What happened to edgy?" I asked, stunned.

"You're doing great," he said, avoiding my question. "Oh, and Josh says hello."

Thank God I'd kept my day job! My head was spinning. I didn't get that job either.

Every year at the holiday party, Hank would say something nice about each of us. For two years in a row, he'd looked at me from the podium and dead panned, "Amanda, how many kids do you have now, twenty?!" He always got a good laugh from the crowd. Funny, right? Not really.

Something else about Hank: During the years I worked for him, he met my husband, Rob, no less than a dozen times. Still, every time he saw him, he'd extend his hand and say, "Hank Shine here. What's your name?" Rob was simply invisible to the man, year after year. We still run into him once a year at Christmastime at our neighborhood tree lighting ceremony on Park Avenue. He seems to vaguely remember me. Maybe I was the one that got away after all?

◦⑤

The Pomegranate

I 'm standing at the kitchen counter. The pomegranate sits on my white plastic cutting board. I take a sharp knife and, holding the orb-shaped fruit steady, carve into it cleanly. Immediately its crimson juice begins to flow. The cutting board looks like a crime scene already. The juice looks like blood; so bright, so red. First, I cut the pomegranate in half, then quarters. I take a section with my bare hands and break through the fibrous middle, full of rinds and sheaths, exposing the colonies of tart, juicy seeds inside. Slowly and surely, I begin the painstaking process of releasing each seed from its cluster. First, I remove the thin, opaque membranes, so bitter to the taste. Underneath lie the seeds. Each makes a satisfying snap as it's released from its individual cluster. I remove each seed one by one and place it in a clear Pyrex bowl. My hands are stained. I feel like Lady Macbeth, "*Out, damned spot!*"

I settle in as I'm working, as deseeding a pomegranate takes time. As I do, my mind wanders back to a time when I wouldn't eat a pomegranate seed or drink its juice. For many years I wouldn't dare. It would have tempted fate. It could have been disastrous; fatal, like before.

It happened in 2000. I was single and living in New York City. I was standing at a different kitchen counter with another glorious pomegranate. I hadn't bought one in a long time, perhaps because I viewed them as a luxury. They are relatively expensive but more than that, they are intimidating. After all, they are the stuff of masterpiece still life paintings. They are also historic, ancient symbols of fertility. Or perhaps I hadn't bought one because of the time needed to prepare it and the mess. In any event, this time I succumbed. And, after preparing it, I sat down and ate the entire thing. I couldn't linger though, as I had an appointment.

I had to take my beloved eight-year-old tabby cat, Alfredo, to the vet for his annual checkup. He was the nervous type, and I usually had to trick him into getting into his travel carrier for the rare trip to the vet. This time, I slid him into it while he was sleeping. He woke up immediately and looked upset as he peered out of the perforated side panels of the carrier. I jostled him a bit getting him out of the apartment. Once we were securely in a yellow taxi heading to our destination, I unzipped the top of the carrier and he lifted his head out of the bag.

He looked around anxiously.

"Don't worry Alfredo, we are on our way," I said soothingly. I pet his head. His orange fur was soft, and his little nose was the color of a pale pink rose.

Suddenly he gasped. I turned his head towards me. His pupils were large and frozen. He was limp.

"Alfredo, Alfredo!" I started to cry. "Oh my God! No, please no."

My world felt like it stopped. We were stuck in traffic on 57th street. My mind raced. I needed to get help immediately. My Alfredo was very ill; maybe even dying; maybe even *dead*. I had to get him to a veterinarian but his was too far away. There wasn't time to get there with the traffic jam.

"Emergency! Emergency!" I yelled to the driver. "I think my cat had a heart attack. Please stop the cab, I've got to get out."

I throw money at the driver and ran out with Alfredo in the bag.

"Help someone!" I was in a panic. I was turning in a circle on the sidewalk trying to get someone to stop and help me. "Does anyone know where a vet is?" A stranger stopped and directed me to a clinic a few blocks away. I ran as fast as I could. I opened the door to the office and raced to the desk breathless.

"Help me please, help me. My cat collapsed in the taxi," I pleaded. "Please hurry, I think he's dying!"

A technician behind the desk grabbed Alfredo and hurried to the back. I sat in the waiting room reeling with disbelief.

What had happened? I remember thinking there was something wrong with the universe. In my mind's eye, I replayed the moment from telescoping perspectives like I'd seen on Sesame Street as a child. First, I saw the two of us in the cab from above. Then my view expanded to an aerial view of the taxi in the middle of traffic on 57th. Then the lens got even wider and the island of Manhattan came into focus. Then the continent, and finally planet earth. When it reached its zenith, it reversed back to Alfredo lying motionless in my arms.

"Miss, miss!" The vet's voice broke my train of thought. He was touching my shoulder gently. I hadn't heard him. I was lost in a mental loop, trying to reverse time.

"I'm so terribly sorry," he said. "There was nothing we could do."

I registered his words but sat frozen.

"Please come with me if you'd like to see him," he said. "What was his name?"

"Alfredo," I said.

I followed into a treatment room, and there on the exam table lay my Alfredo.

I collapsed in tears rubbing my face in his fur, cuddling his lifeless body.

"Alfredo had a stroke or a heart attack," the vet said. "He died immediately. We tried to revive him but couldn't. I'm so sorry."

"I could perform an autopsy," he said. "So, you can find out what happened."

I declined. It didn't matter why it happened. He was gone. Gone forever. I arranged for cremation in a daze of grief and left his body there.

That day, my life changed. Never before had I witnessed death, let alone the shock of an unforeseen death. In middle school, I had lost a grandfather in his eighties. I'd also lost family pets through the years, but the grief was shared. Not this time. Alfredo was *mine*. The randomness of this loss reverberated in my body and soul. My mind struggled to find causation and meaning. I blamed myself for placing Alfredo in the carrier bag while he was sleeping. I attributed the attack to his not having had the time to adjust to the sudden change of environment. My grief also led me to create a theory of cause and effect: my eating the pomegranate had caused his death. I was sure of it. Naturally, the only way to avoid this ever happening again was never to eat one.

While part of me knew this was crazy, another part of me needed to feel in control. Thus, for the next fifteen years, I never touched a pomegranate. During this time, I adopted a pug puppy named Milo. Milo lived thirteen years, in my mind because I never ate a pomegranate. Milo did suffer many medical ailments, but he didn't die suddenly and unexpectedly like Alfredo.

Several years after Milo's death, while grocery shopping, I stopped at a display of beautiful pomegranates. I longed to taste one again. *Take a chance*, I told myself. *You don't have any pets right now so you're safe.* So, I did take a chance, and another and another thereafter. I now have a six-year-old King Charles spaniel name Toby, and I am still eating pomegranates. While the fear lingers, I haven't stopped. Maybe it's because I'm older and have now lost many people that I've loved, even when I wasn't eating pomegranates. Or maybe it's because I've become better at tolerating the uncertainty that is life. Or maybe it's because I've become more of a risk taker. I would be lying if I said I didn't think about Alfredo and death sometimes when I eat one, but now the taste also reminds me of life.

❦

'Til Death Do Us Part

Last week my husband, Rob, and I drove through the town of Brattleboro, Vermont on our way to our family ski house at Stratton Mountain. We don't always drive that route, but we had stopped off in Deerfield, Massachusetts to visit our sons at boarding school there. It was a lovely day for a drive, cold and clear. As the passenger, I had the chance to look out the window on the way and see rolling fields covered in snow, mountains of densely packed trees, and crystal-clear babbling streams partially frozen with crystalline ice.

As we neared the town, my eyes lingered on the quaint, old buildings. Then we passed the courthouse. I knew it well. I'd spent a month there in 2006 covering a murder trial for Court Television Network.

The case was unusual in one respect: the alleged murderer was a 73-year-old wife, mother and librarian. Hope Schreiner was accused of killing her 78-year-old husband, Robert. He was found dead in their driveway from a brutal head wound. The medical examiner also found large doses of the sedative Ambien in his blood.

At trial, the evidence revealed some key things: Robert Schreiner had been ill with lung cancer; the defendant, Hope, had taken to sleeping with an elderly bachelor who lived nearby; Hope was tired of taking care of her husband, and after 43 years of marriage, she'd had enough.

Hope said she discovered Robert bleeding from the head in their driveway after returning from running errands. The murder weapon was a pronged instrument that was never found, likely the couples' potato hoe. Incriminating DNA evidence and blood were found in the home. Also, ten witnesses took the stand, painting a devastating picture for Hope.

Two friends testified that Hope told them she was tired of taking care of Robert. She allegedly also admitted, "I just snapped." She reportedly told another witness she'd, "put Ambien in his morning coffee that day." Finally, in response to a friend's concern about a killer on the loose in Vermont, she'd allegedly responded, "Don't worry. I did it."

The trial tore the family apart. It was a "melded" family of nine children (eight of whom were from their previous marriages). Only one child was from their current marriage, a son. One of Hope's daughters testified against her mother. For her having "crossed enemy lines," she was completely blackballed by her mother and her maternal siblings. The victim's children testified to the cruelty and selfishness of their stepmother. Only the couple's youngest son, an adult at the time, supported his mother and sat beside her during trial.

Watching the trial, two things struck me in particular. One was the testimony of the elderly lover. He sheepishly confessed to the affair and said he felt bad about it because he'd known and liked the deceased. He said it was, "just sex" to him. He testified he didn't love

Hope and never would have married her. He also said he wouldn't have entered into the relationship had the victim not been ill and unaware. Sitting in court that day listening to that testimony, I felt sorry for her. Pity was not an emotion I felt very often for alleged murderers; however, putting her alleged act aside, I did feel it. She was hearing from the witness stand that she was not loved by the man she'd been sleeping with. I believe it was likely the passion of that romance that prompted her to kill her husband in the first place. The testimony clearly showed that she wanted another life. I recall thinking she was likely in love with her neighbor, and that her nightly treks across her field to his house provided her with excitement and a sense of escape from the grim reality at home. I wondered why she didn't wait for her husband to die of cancer. By all accounts she had a good life including weekly tennis games with girlfriends, her work, and a very gentlemanly husband. But obviously it wasn't enough for her; and in my experience it rarely is for people who end up on trial for murder.

The other thing that has stayed with me all these years was seeing Hope's son stand by her while she was on trial. The evidence was weighted heavily against her; yet he said he believed in her innocence. He also appeared to provide her with reassuring comfort and unconditional love throughout the proceedings. Boys can be naïve, more naïve than girls in my opinion. In this case, the man's father died by his mother's hand -- yet he still held hers. I wonder how he feels today, thirteen years later?

Postscript: The trial ended with Schreiner being convicted of 2nd degree murder. She was sentenced to 17 years to life in prison. At the time, Schreiner was Vermont's oldest female inmate.

You Get Wrinkles When You Worry

You get wrinkles when you worry, so don't worry!"

Jean looked at me and smiled. Her blue eyes twinkled within the frames of her Gloria-Steinem sized, pink glasses. Her soft white hair framed her heart-shaped face. She had pale skin and wore pink lipstick. Jean was in her late sixties. Hers was a kind face. She lived life with curiosity, humor and good will. She was a "glass half full" person; optimistic and positive.

"Okay, Jean. I'll try," I said meekly, wishing I could be as carefree as she was.

Not worrying came naturally for her. For me, it wasn't that easy. Mine were the garden-variety worries of a college co-ed: school and relationships. I usually had some tangled nugget of anxiety I was attempting to tease out. Talking to her calmed me. Plus, she made me laugh. She was full of fun.

"I really was a femme fatale, Amanda. Back then I was gorgeous and thin, just like you! Get the photos for her David! Tell her."

"Oh yes, Jean was a dish," David added, smiling shyly. David was Jean's husband. They were opposites: he tall, thin and reserved; she, short, stout and extraverted. Invariably, out would come photos of Jean in the 40s and 50s; then, those of David looking dashing in uniform. I delighted in them all, and in the stories that went with them. Afternoon visits to their Chicago home often turned into dinners. Jean was a fantastic cook and insisted on feeding me all kinds of delicious and homey things whenever I visited. She was like a sweet, funny Grandmother you felt comfortable with. Although she never had children of her own, she was a stepmom to David's daughter from a prior marriage and delighted in their grandchildren. She made me feel like family too. She would always hug me tight and tell me how happy she was to see me. Many a cold, winter's night was spent in the warmth of their home and company.

Spring brought other adventures. Jean and I would often walk around their neighborhood in the Lincoln Park section of Chicago. Jean was constantly greeting, or being greeted by, someone she knew. Shopkeepers, neighbors walking their dogs, even the random delivery person knew her. She projected a sort of small town, genuine affection for others. She was generous of spirit.

Walks were never just walks either; they were treasure hunts. Often, she paused on the sidewalk to examine some tissue paper poking out of a garbage can.

"Nice!" she would say, stopping to pull out the piece that had caught her eye. She'd smooth it out on her paint-splotched pants and fold it into a neat square before putting it into her tote bag. I kept my eye out for interesting pieces of tissue paper too. Jean would incorporate them into her work.

Jean was an artist. She'd been painting her whole life at the Chicago Art Institute. She painted primarily portraits and still lives. Later in life she'd begun adding tissue paper to her paintings and making collages. They looked a bit impressionistic as a result; the softness of the tissue paper layered on top or within them.

Visiting Jean and David was easy. I'd hop on the L Train in Evanston and in less than thirty minutes I'd be squirreled away in their cozy townhouse. It was full of wonderful kitchen smells, art, books, and dogs (theirs and others). It was a narrow townhouse with a metal, spiral staircase leading up to the upper floor.

I first met Jean and David in 1983, when I enrolled as a freshman at Northwestern University. My parents introduced us. Jean and David had rented my parents an apartment in Chicago when they moved there in the 1960s. At that time, my dad was doing a medical residency at Northwestern and my mom was an undergraduate at the University of Chicago. Jean liked to tell me the story of the day my mom walked into the rental apartment. Jean said my mom took one step inside, looked around and said, "I'll take it." I always pictured mom as Mary Tyler Moore in that moment, spinning around with a smile on her face before throwing her hat in the air and making her decision.

It was a great decision; they were great people. During college, they became my go-to couple. I brought every single boyfriend I had at Northwestern to meet them without fail. Everyone loved them.

I treated Jean and David as surrogate grandparents. Once, I became faint while visiting the Art Institute. I called them right away and David came and got me. Conveniently, a nice young doctor name Kevin had moved into the townhouse next door. They called him and he came right over to make sure I was okay; I was, but ended up spending night at Jean and David's house anyway. I felt safe and comfortable with them.

When I graduated, Jean gave me my favorite painting right off her wall. It's of a beautiful, redheaded girl looking out a window. It has held pride of place in every home I've had since. After graduation, I kept in touch with them. When Jean died, more than twenty years later, it was a great loss. I went to visit David. It was painful to sit together in the house without Jean. He gave me photos of them when I left. We spoke regularly after that. Eventually he moved into a nursing home. His death two years ago left me sadder than when my own grandfather died.

"I've lived too long, Amanda. Everything hurts," David told me not long before he passed. "I want you to keep in touch with my granddaughter," he said. "You're both lovely, lovely people. I love you."

"I love you too, David," I said near tears.

I still do.

The Scarlet "A"

Dani, our babysitter, startles me by opening the door almost simultaneously with my turning the key in the lock. I was returning home around 4 p.m. on a school day.

"Oh Dani, hi," I say, surprised.

"Hi Amanda," she says sheepishly, whispering. "Let's go back outside for a minute." She says this quickly, glancing back over her shoulder into the apartment. At the same time, she's rushing me out the door to the elevator landing.

"What's wrong?" I say, concerned.

"Nothing really, but I wanted talk to you without the boys hearing."

"Why?"

"Well, they had a conversation you should know about. We were all sitting at the kitchen table after school."

"Okay," I said feeling impatient.

"So, the boys were eating their snack and Grey says to Ford, 'I know a secret.' And then Ford says to Grey, 'What secret?' And then Grey said to Ford, 'A secret about Mom.' Then Ford says to Grey, 'What about Mom?'"

As Dani recounts the conversation she's turning her head left to right, back and forth, like she's watching a tennis match.

She continues: "So then Grey says, 'Mom was married before!' Then Ford says, 'No way!' Then Grey says, 'Way!' Then Ford says, 'How do you know?' Then Grey says, 'Mom told me.' Then Ford says, 'She didn't tell me.' Then Grey says, 'It's on the internet.'"

"They asked *me* if *I* knew, but I said I didn't, because I don't!" Dani said dramatically.

"Thanks Dani. I really appreciate your telling me this. Yes, it's true. It just came up this morning. Do the boys seem upset?"

"Grey does, but Ford just seems surprised he didn't know too."

"Okay, I've got this," I said.

The boys were now in 3rd and 4th grade; eight and nine years old, respectively.

The whole thing started that morning when Grey, my older son, asked me about his name being in the papers when he was born. I'd been a television reporter and anchor in New York City at that time, so his birth made the news. I went online to show him and the first story that came up was my marriage announcement. Even though it was off topic, he saw it and wanted to read it. It ended with, "the bride's first marriage ended in divorce." Grey turned to me and said, "So *Grandma* was divorced?"

I knew this day would come eventually but I'd dreaded it. Even when the topic came up about *other* kids' parents getting divorced at their grade school, I'd never mentioned my own. I didn't even tell other moms at their school that I'd been married before, for fear it would get back to my boys. I worried my sons would look at me differently after hearing I'd had another husband. I wasn't sure how to explain it to them. I felt embarrassed and ashamed seeing myself through their eyes. Now the moment of truth was here. I took a deep breath.

I looked at Grey and simply said, "No, *I* was."

He looked perplexed.

"That's right, Grey. Sometimes people marry young and it doesn't work out. I married a very nice man I went to law school with when I was twenty-five. We were great friends, but in the end, I realized I wasn't married to the right person. It was the right decision, because otherwise I wouldn't have met your dad and had you. Do you see what I mean?"

"I guess so," he said, still looking confused.

"Your dad waited a long time to get married. People are different. Sometimes they know right away and sometimes they don't."

"I don't want to hear anymore," Grey said suddenly exasperated. He was covering his ears with his hands and shaking his head. He looked like Macaulay Culkin in the movie poster for *Home Alone*.

I realized I'd said too much. I needed to wrap the conversation up *pronto.*

"Okay honey. I love you very much."

I gave him a hug and a kiss, and he scurried away. I sat down on my bed, crestfallen. I felt my reputation was tarnished in Grey's eyes, and that I was going to go down in history as a wanton woman while Rob, my husband, who had years of wild and crazy bachelorhood, would get off scot-free. It wasn't fair! I felt I had the equivalent of a scarlet letter on my chest.

And now, just a few hours later, Grey had already shared the news with Ford and Dani! I walked into the apartment trying to decide how best to explain things to Ford. I needn't have worried though: when I did, he barely looked up from his Lego.

"Do you have any questions, Ford?" I asked.

"No mom, I'm good. Can I watch TV?"

"Sure," I said, reaching out to hug him tight. "I love you."

Eight years have passed since that day. Neither son has mentioned it since.

Maybe the "Scarlet A" has faded from my chest. Maybe it now stands for Amanda.

Fit For Framing

S tarting in grade school, I was often asked to draw things for teachers. They must have noticed I had an affinity for it during class projects.

"Amanda, please do a poster of a pilgrim for our Thanksgiving study week," Ms. Vaughn, my kindergarten teacher said, smiling brightly while gesturing towards a crafts table set with white poster boards and rainbow-colored ink pens.

"Amanda, could you draw something to hang on the wall for our Columbus Day celebration?" Mrs. Jenkins, my third-grade teacher asked. She was ultimately delighted with my depiction of the explorer and his three ships: The Niña, the Pinta and the Santa Maria.

I liked the attention. I always received complements from other teachers and my classmates. It was fun to see my work displayed in the classroom too. I'd never taken any art classes; I just had some innate ability.

Like most of my talents that appeared at a young age, my parents ignored them. Not intentionally, I'm sure. Maybe my teachers didn't inform my parents? Or maybe my parents, like many parents in the 60s and 70s, just didn't focus on me enough to see the potential. Or perhaps being a "left-brained" lawyer (my mom) and doctor (my dad), they didn't value my "right-brain" talents?

All I know for sure is that they weren't like I am as a parent: if I see a spark of interest or ability, I fan that flame until my boys beg me to stop. In my wake are all kinds of enrichment classes I've signed them up for; some stuck, others didn't, but my boys can never say they didn't get the chance to try, or that their budding talents were overlooked. I was determined not to make the same mistakes my parents made.

Thus, my modest artistic talents lay dormant for many years. My first real fine arts class was drawing in Florence, Italy, during a semester abroad my junior year of college. I'd dropped out of a literature course called, "Sexuality in the Renaissance," because I found reading and discussing erotic texts embarrassing. You can therefore imagine my chagrin when I transferred into a beginning drawing class instead, and found myself staring at a nude, male model. For weeks, all of my sketches lacked a certain organ. In time I got over it.

When I worked as an attorney and later as a journalist, from time to time I would sign up for a drawing class at night. I liked the art school atmosphere: the multi-generational students, the casualness of the clothing, and the serenity and silence of the studios. I liked being able to focus without distraction.

When I stopped working as a television journalist in 2006, the first thing I did was sign up for a beginning painting class at the Art Students League in New York City. The class met three times a week in the mornings. I dove right in, learning all I could. After that class, I took another painting class, then another. I settled into a rhythm with a wonderful teacher and later followed her to the National Academy School of Art. There, I took classes five mornings a week from 9 to 12. My boys were young, and the schedule worked for us. I'd get them ready for school and drop them off before heading to painting class. After class, I had time to run errands before picking them up.

Painting fit with my detail-oriented personality. I loved working on a portrait until I was satisfied. I'd often be mulling over a nose or an eye while lying in bed at night. I just couldn't wait to get up and 'massage' it more and get it just right. Oil paints can be added to, removed and modified. It was a perfect medium for me.

During the six years I painted full-time, I completed at least fifty paintings, including still lifes, landscapes, and portraits. Friends often encouraged me to sell them, as did my husband, who was concerned with the diminishing storage space in our home. But my painting wasn't something I wanted to become a business. I'd worked for years and did not want my avocation to turn into a vocation. Despite my feelings, I did sell a handful of paintings to friends who insisted. I also gifted paintings to members of my family, extended family, and best friends.

A highlight was being asked to donate a painting to an important charity auction. My piece hung next to one by the famous painter Jasper Johns at The Children's Cancer and Blood Foundation Art Exhibit and Sale, which took place at Sotheby's in 2011. My painting sold for $3,000.

Another highlight: One day I was carrying a completed canvas home down Park Avenue. It was a relatively large painting, four feet by six feet, of my husband in Les Baux de Provence, France. It had a big sky, big landscape, John Wayne-type of appeal. A portly doctor in his lab coat was smoking a cigarette outside his office as I walked by.

"Hey, wait a minute!" He said. "Can I see that painting?"

"Sure," I said. "I painted it."

He gave the painting a long look, walking back and forth on the sidewalk and stepping in closer and then out again. My arms were getting tired.

"I love it! Can I buy it?" He asked.

"Oh, that's so nice," I said, surprised. "But it's of my husband in France and I want to keep it."

"Well, if you change your mind, will you call me? I'll give you my card." He began searching in his pocket and ultimately handed me a crinkled business card.

"Sure, I said. Thanks, I'm flattered."

When I recounted the conversation to my husband, Rob, that night, his response was unequivocal:

"Sell it!" He exclaimed enthusiastically.

"Of course, I won't," I said, a bit taken back by his lack of sentimentality.

"This is something our grandkids will keep, and know that their grandmother painted it of their grandfather. I can't believe you'd sell it."

"Just paint another one," he said crossing his arms, as though that solved the problem.

"I can't just whip these things out!" I said. "Humph."

The painting now hangs in the 'man cave' of our home in Southampton, a testament to my love for Rob and to his misplaced pragmatism.

How I Met Your Father or
Passage from India

I t all began in January 2000, with an Indian lunch at
a tiny restaurant in New York's East Village. I was
seated alone at a table for two in the middle of the room
enjoying a selection of my favorites: papadam, samosa
with yogurt sauce, tandoori chicken and saag paneer.
During this time an Indian man was seated right next to
me, eating. He looked around my age, was clean-cut, and
friendly. Within minutes, he began to chat with me about
the restaurant, my selections and the like.

His name was Raj. When I said my name, he smiled
warmly.

"I knew it," he said. "I watch you on CNBC Business
News!"

Raj worked as a stockbroker at a Wall Street firm.
He was engaging and personable. I wasn't attracted to
him physically, but liked his energy and thought he could
be a fun friend. Before I left, we exchanged numbers and
talked about perhaps having another Indian meal in the
future.

A few days later, I met Raj for a drink at the St. Regis
Hotel after work. We had a good time. He was a social
butterfly and introduced me to people he knew at the
bar. After an hour, he asked if I'd like to join him for
dinner with a group of his friends that night. I said yes,
why not?

When we arrived at the restaurant, Le Bilboquet, there were eight men waiting at a large round table; all of them were old friends and worked in finance. They also watched CNBC regularly. I'm sure they were as surprised to find me there, as I was to be there. I noticed a quiet, preppy-looking man in a pale pink button-down shirt sitting across the table. He was tall and slim, with light brown hair and blue eyes. We didn't speak to each other at dinner; he was seated too far away, and the restaurant was noisy.

Following dinner our group moved on for drinks to Le Charlot, another popular bar/restaurant nearby. After about twenty minutes, I slipped outside for some fresh air. I couldn't take all the cigarette smoke in the bar. I was standing just outside the door, watching the snow fall on the sidewalk and breathing in the cool, crisp air.

"Hi. Are you okay?"

I turned to find the man in the pink button-down shirt from our table standing beside me. "I'm Rob Holmén."

"Oh yes, thanks Rob. I'm fine. It's just too smoky in there for me. I needed a break," I said, smiling at him. It was thoughtful of him to check on me. He was soft-spoken and polite. He asked how I knew Raj and I told him Raj was a new acquaintance I'd just met at an Indian restaurant while having lunch.

"Are you coming dancing with us at Au Bar?" He asked.

"No. I have a new pug puppy at home, and I really need to walk him."

He asked me about my puppy, and where I lived.

"Why don't I go with you to walk your dog, and then we can come back uptown and rejoin the group?" Rob suggested.

I thought about it and decided that sounded fun. "Sure, that would be nice." I said. At that time, I lived in the West Village. It was a long trip there and back, but I was enjoying myself.

When we finally arrived at the dance club, Raj seemed upset with me. I hadn't realized he thought of me as his date. Rob whispered in my ear, "I wouldn't worry about it. You know, he's married with children. He'll get over it."

"I did *not* know that," I said, grateful for the information. "He never mentioned it." I stopped worrying about Raj. Rob and I danced the night away and, as the saying goes, the rest is history.

The Competitive Spirit

There's nothing my sons love more than a spirited competition. No matter what activity one can think of, be it tennis, basketball, word games, charades, monopoly, test scores or grades, it's just that much more fun if they're competing against each other or someone else. They've been this way since they were little; now they're fifteen and sixteen. They are serious competitors yet, at the same time, good-natured. I've observed this phenomenon with wonder, like an anthropologist staring at a rare species and trying to sort out its origin. How can it actually be more fun to compete than to simply do the activity collaboratively? Since having children, I've noticed more than ever that many people share this love of competition. I've had to face the fact that it is I who am the rare species, not they.

Why is it that I shudder at even the word competition? It stems from the way I was raised or perhaps my erroneous interpretations of the world around me as I grew. My parents never played any competitive sports during our childhood, alone, together or with us. We didn't even play games as a family. My father once famously declared that even watching television should be done alone. "No communal TV!" was his motto. We did enjoy meals and trips together, as well as activities like going to plays, sporting events and movies, but nothing involved our competing with each other. That's not to say we children weren't competitive with each other. We were a family of competitive people and individually strove to achieve our respective goals. Some of my goals clashed with those of my siblings. For example, we competed for our parents' attention. I also competed with my older sister and she with me; not in a healthy way, but in secret from the time we were little. I felt I wasn't supposed to feel competitive; that it was mean, or wrong to want to do better than she did. I hid my competitive nature by not overtly competing against her, but at the same time working hard to measure up on looks and achievements. I was jealous of her without a socially acceptable outlet for that feeling.

My sister didn't seem to suffer from a fear of competing. I remember she played in tennis matches and swim races at our club when she was in junior high. On the rare occasions I remember playing tennis with her, she always won. I felt embarrassed and resentful. I took losses personally and didn't like the person who'd won as much as before. I don't ever remember a parent, coach or friend ever talking to me about competition. If they had, I might have learned that competition is important: it teaches someone how to win and how to lose gracefully. It's an essential life skill. Even if I didn't enjoy competing one-on-one, being on any kind of team would have taught me valuable lessons.

In my careers, as an attorney and later as a television journalist, I would have been better able to handle the stresses of work had I been a better competitor. Instead of rolling with the punches, I often felt beaten up. I felt anger and resentment towards colleagues who got the promotions or jobs I wanted. If only I'd learned that competition is different from jealousy. The former is healthy; the latter is not. I wish I'd been a more gracious loser; not only externally but also internally where it counted more.

My struggles continue. I absolutely love playing in tennis clinics and enjoy the camaraderie. But as soon as we start playing games, I feel tense. Even when I win, I worry that the loser won't like me. It's even worse if I lose. Then I worry that the winner won't want to play with me again. Recently, my husband suggested we play together in a club mixed-doubles tournament. Although I enjoy our weekly clinic together, I told him no. The idea was just too stressful. Maybe next year.

In the meantime, my boys continue to be my best teachers and role models. When we play tennis as a family, they make me laugh with their ribbing and swagger! They'll don headbands and make aggressive gestures in jest, just to get a laugh. Like a sports psychologist, I like to get inside their heads whenever possible. I've taken to asking what they're thinking of at various moments during play.

"What are you thinking of when you're serving?" I'll ask my partner mid-game. Or "What should *I* be thinking of now that the pressure is on and we're losing?"

"Just think, 'You're going down!'" Grey, my older son, tells me conspiratorially.

"Mom, just think to yourself, 'I'm just soooo much better than you are!'" Ford, my younger son, advises.

I just stop and stare at them in absolute awe. Where do they get it?

Fascinating!

Kidding Around

"Ford, what would you like to know about me? As you know, I'm in a memoir class and I thought I would answer a question you're curious about this week and write about it."

I'm texting my younger son, who is a freshman in high school at Deerfield Academy in Massachusetts. I'm at home in New York City.

"What you did for fun as a kid/what you did that you remember. Or why you decided to move uptown in New York," he texts back. I ponder his suggestions before replying.

"Thanks. Moved uptown because I married your dad! I'll do the first one. Can I start at [the] youngest age? Up to what age?" I ask.

"Doesn't matter. Maybe like grade school," he responds.

While it sounds like a simple task, I must admit I'm stumped. Where do I begin? Perhaps at the beginning, growing up in Hillsborough, California in the 1960s?

I could start by telling Ford about my having gone to an unusual pre-nursery school when I was three, where they had live Guinea pigs that we could dress up and wheel around in tiny strollers. I loved their soft fur and twitching noses. I really liked wheeling my furry pretend babies around too, usually while they sported a feather boa or felt hat.

Or maybe I'll share with him my earliest memories of nursery school at The Little French School. It had huge sand boxes in the back yard with lots of shovels and pails. That's where I met my lifelong friend Christian. Every day, the old French lady who ran the school would ring a little bell and we'd line up single file for apple juice. We also sang French nursery rhymes like "Alouette." I really liked it there.

Or perhaps I'll tell Ford about Kindergarten at North Hillsborough School, where they had an extensive playground. I loved playing hopscotch with my friends. We used chalk to draw numbers in the squares and compete -- yes, compete! – at recess. I also loved playing tetherball, which is a like a volleyball attached to a rope that wraps around a center pole. Running, skipping and jumping rope were also favorite pastimes. We had individual jump ropes, as well as extra-long ones. Two girls would each hold an end and start swinging. Then we'd take turns running in and out of the ropes while jumping and keeping the rhythm. Hula hoops were in the mix too. Playgrounds were always one of my favorite places.

Possibly, I'll write about riding my bike with my friend Sally when I was in grade school. She and I loved to ride our bikes. It was great fun and always an adventure. Our favorite destination was a sandwich shop about a mile away in the neighboring town of Burlingame. There, we would order our favorite sandwich: Italian salami, provolone cheese, with lots of mayo, on a roll – heated. Next stop: giant Coke Slurpees at the local Seven-Eleven. Looking back, Sally and I had tons of fun (and ate a lot of calories).

Perhaps I should also tell Ford about all the exciting sleepovers I had in grade school? We'd usually make forts out of blankets and sheets and crawl around on our hands and knees with flashlights. I remember secret missions crawling under my sister's bed in the dark while she was sleeping, trying not to laugh and failing miserably! As we got older, my friends and I would bake a lot of chocolate chip cookies, try on makeup, and do our nails when they slept over. We also had large slumber parties when I was in middle school, where we'd spend all night talking, playing board games (including *Séance* where you'd attempt to make contact with spirits of the dead), singing "Mr. Postman," and making prank phone calls, (which are practical jokes on the person answering, in case you haven't made one.)

Certainly, I'll tell Ford how I loved to go to the movies. My favorite part was getting a bucket of popcorn with extra butter. In middle school, my friend Christian and I each bought our own bucket and would sometime see double features. That, after a Chinese food lunch! When we couldn't get a ride to the restaurant or to the movies, we'd walked there because we were too young to drive. This seems a good time to add that I was always thin despite how much I ate, probably because I was always very active.

I can't leave out telling Ford about birthday parties, can I? In middle school, roller-skating was really popular. I still remember going round and round endlessly with a disco ball scattering lights across the ceiling and loud music pulsing in my ears. They always served Hostess Ho Hos and Ding Dongs as snacks. I didn't love roller skating, but I never missed a party. I was always social, and enjoyed being with my friends.

In fact, when I think about the things I did for fun as a kid, they almost always involved spending time with my friends. Even reading books was best shared; my friend Anneliese and I read dozens of Barbara Cartland romance novels growing up, passing them back and forth and discussing them at length.

I think it's important to share with Ford that life was different when I was a kid primarily because we didn't have personal electronic devices. When it came to entertainment technology, we had record players, radios, and television. When I was very young, I watched *Mr. Roger's Neighborhood*, and *Sesame Street*, daily. A few years after that, I watched *I Dream of Jeannie*, and *I Love Lucy*. As I grew older, my favorite TV shows included: *The Brady Bunch*, *The Partridge Family*, *The Mary Tyler Moore Show*, and *The Courtship of Eddy's Father*. Friday nights were the best. My mom let us eat Swanson TV dinners, which consisted of a pre-made frozen dinner you baked in the oven. The container had separate compartments: one for fried chicken, one for peas, one for mashed potatoes, and one for, my favorite, the brownie dessert.

Like you, dear Ford, I always liked to save the best bit for last.

❧